D1262065

Ed King's
MISSISSIPPI

Behind the Scenes of Freedom Summer

REV. ED KING AND TRENT WATTS

UNIVERSITY PRESS OF MISSISSIPPI • JACKSON

www.upress.state.ms.us

The University Press of Mississippi is a member of the Association of American University Presses.

All photograph captions are transcriptions of Rev. Ed King's handwritten notes on the backs of the photographs. Ed King Collection, Mississippi Department of Archives and History, Jackson, Mississippi. PI/1984.0018/Box 57/Folder 1.

First printing 2014

∞

Library of Congress Cataloging-in-Publication Data

King, Ed, Rev., 1936–
Ed King's Mississippi : behind the scenes of freedom summer / Rev. Ed King and Trent Watts.
pages cm.
Includes index.
ISBN 978-1-62846-115-2 (cloth : alk. paper) — ISBN 978-1-62846-116-9 (ebook)
1. African Americans—Civil rights—Mississippi—History—20th century.
2. Civil rights movements—Mississippi—History—20th century.
3. Mississippi—Race relations—History—20th century. 4. King, Ed, Rev., 1936–
5. Civil rights workers—Mississippi—Biography. I. Watts, Trent, 1965– II. Title.
III. Title: Behind the scenes of freedom summer.
E185.93.M6K46 2014
323.092—dc23
[B]   2014010367
British Library Cataloging-in-Publication Data available

For my father, Wayne Edward Brown

TW

CONTENTS

ACKNOWLEDGMENTS

I DEEPLY APPRECIATE THE SUPPORT AND ENCOURAGEMENT OF FAMILY and friends, especially my brother, Alan; my physician friend, Dr. Robert Smith; the Rev. Sam Tomlinson; Todd Pyles; Les Dunbar; Dr. Ham Benghuzzi and Dr. Jessica Bailey, of the School of Health Related Professions of the University of Mississippi Medical Center; Craig Gill and staff of the University Press of Mississippi; and my co-author, Dr. Trent Watts, who had the original concept for this kind of book.

This book is dedicated to we few, we happy few, we band of brothers and sisters, on the way to the Promised Land, to Freedom Land, and to the Beloved Community.

EK

WRITING THIS BOOK HAS BEEN A GREAT PLEASURE. I THANK THE MANY people who were generous with their assistance, their friendship, or both. Craig Gill at the University Press of Mississippi has been supportive, patient, and encouraging since I told him about this project several years ago at a Mississippi Historical Society meeting in Jackson. He, John Langston, and others at the press have made me want to work with them again, and I hope to have the opportunity to do that with future projects. Readers of the manuscript offered valuable suggestions for improvements. I hope that I have made good use of their many useful comments and recommendations. Thanks also to Anne Stascavage and Carol Cox.

At the Missouri University of Science and Technology, students Trista Bruning, Courtney Rose, Augusta Turner, Cassie Rizzo, and Sherry Smith supplied valuable assistance. Special thanks to Stephanee Walker for her diligent work. Also here at Missouri S & T, colleagues and librarians have made work easier and life in general more pleasant. At the Curtis Laws Wilson Library, Marsha Fuller, June Snell, Chris Jocius, Mary Haig, and Sherry Mahnken were great at helping me obtain books and other material. Chris pointed me toward many relevant materials that otherwise I would have missed.

In the English Department, Linda Sands always has a smile that makes it nice to come to work. Thanks also to colleagues Kris Swenson and Anne Cotterill for their kind interest in this project and for listening to me talk about it. Jack Morgan, on the other hand, should be ashamed of himself for retiring and moving away. I miss his sense of humor, scholarly example, and broad learning. All of us in the department miss our good friend and colleague John Lemmermann, the loss of whom we still keenly feel.

Scholars writing Mississippi history are fortunate to be able to work in the William F. Winter Archives and History Building in Jackson, home of the Mississippi Department of Archives and History. Archivists and librarians there provided much support for this project. When I asked Anne Webster if she knew how I might locate Rev. Ed King, she suggested that I should look near her on Sunday mornings in Jackson's Galloway Memorial United Methodist Church. Thanks as well to Hank Holmes, Grady Howell, Clinton Bagley, and Celia Tisdale. Clarence Hunter deserves special recognition, too, for his work in caring for the MDAH's invaluable collection of Tougaloo College civil rights–related material. I also wish to thank Ainsley Powell and Pamela Williamson for their assistance at the J. D. Williams Library at the University of Mississippi, a campus I never tire of visiting.

My greatest debt is of course to Rev. Edwin King himself. He has offered enthusiastic assistance and guidance and was generous with his time while I prepared this manuscript. For that help I am most thankful. As a native Mississippian, I am even more grateful for the courage he showed in attempting to open a closed society during the years covered in this book. Growing up in Mississippi in the 1970s and 1980s, I had no idea of the conditions that had prevailed in the 1960s.

I am fortunate to know Steve Reich and Ron Granieri, good historians and even better companions. I also want to thank Lindgren Johnson for her friendship and help during some challenging times. And thanks again to my good friend Vance Poole; a brief word does not begin to acknowledge my debt to him. At the University of Mississippi, Joan Wylie Hall was a masterful, inspiring teacher; her encouragement over the years has been a blessing.

This is the first of my books to have been written since my wife, Jennifer, came into my life. I thank her again for her love and her patience with all my many faults. My children, Jack and Ellie, continue to be sources of great joy. Because of the sacrifices made by Ed King and others in that summer of 1964, the Mississippi that we visit to see their grandparents looks much different from the Mississippi that they will see and read about in this book. Thanks also to my mother for her continued support and love. Finally, I am especially glad to be able to dedicate this book to my father, for whom the year 1964 has special significance.

TW

Ed King's Mississippi

INTRODUCTION

TRENT WATTS

The Lord saw it, and it displeased Him that there was no justice.

ISAIAH 59:15

"THE 'LONG HOT SUMMER' IS ABOUT TO BEGIN," WROTE REV. EDWIN KING, chaplain of Mississippi's Tougaloo College, to a fellow Methodist minister on May 29, 1964.[1] In that summer of 1964, approximately one thousand volunteers—most of them white college students, but their ranks also included doctors, lawyers, and clergy—from California, Ohio, Michigan, New York, and a host of other states came to Mississippi to work with local people and other civil rights activists on what became known as the Freedom Summer project. For three months, movement workers canvassed cotton fields and black neighborhoods urging and instructing people how to register to vote; they lived with local families and built Freedom Schools where black men, women, and children were taught the rudiments of civics as well as black history and art, music, and drama. More broadly, the Freedom Summer project attempted to support the grassroots civil rights movement in the state by encouraging and enabling black Mississippians to claim basic civil rights and a dignity that a Jim Crow society had systematically attempted to deny them.[2]

The Mississippi Summer Project, as the initiative was initially called by movement workers, provoked a scathing, indignant reaction from many white Mississippians, who viewed the civil rights work that summer as nothing less than an invasion. Congressman Thomas G. Abernathy wrote: "Agitators in the civil rights movement, all mature adults, have for months been carefully mapping strategy and tactics for disorder in our State." Governor Paul B. Johnson Jr., who campaigned for election in 1963 largely on his opposition as lieutenant governor to James Meredith's 1962 racial integration of the University of Mississippi, said of the summer project: "We are not going to allow a group of outsiders to come in and drive a wedge into the unity of the state."³ Johnson's conception of "we" was of course limited to the majority of Mississippi's white population; only such a definition allows his assertion of "unity" to be credible, despite most white Mississippians' insistence that race relations in the state were fundamentally sound and mutually acceptable. Not all white Mississippians were Klansmen, of course, and only a small percentage of the state's whites responded to Freedom Summer with overt violence. That said, the threat of violence, as black Mississippians knew, was real and liable to manifest itself without warning. "In this summer," wrote a northern journalist, "the stranger is the enemy, and the men of Mississippi wait and watch for him . . . Every man watches and every man is watched."⁴ Most student volunteers were not naïve about the dangers they faced in the state. One wrote: "Mississippi is going to be hell this summer . . . I'd venture to say that every member of the Mississippi staff has been beaten up at least once and he who has not been shot at is rare."⁵

The state of Mississippi, directly through the Sovereignty Commission, and indirectly through the Citizens' Council, defended racial segregation as the foundation of the "Mississippi way of life." Of the Citizens' Council's influence, historian Charles W. Eagles writes, "By February, 1956, one observer declared that it had 'in fact become the government in Mississippi' and it 'controls the legislative and executive and judicial arms of government.'"⁶ Few white Mississippians spoke openly or publicly in contradiction of the views espoused by those organizations. To have lived in Mississippi during the period from the *Brown* school desegregation decision in 1954 through the Freedom Summer of 1964 was to have heard little from politicians, most newspapers and clergymen, and most of one's

neighbors—if you were white, that is—other than that the state was increasingly the target of atheistic, Communist-inspired race mixers bent upon bringing chaos out of order.⁷ With F.B.I. Director J. Edgar Hoover openly questioning not whether but rather how large a role Communists played in the broader civil rights movement, who could blame an average white Mississippian for thinking the same thing? Given the tenacity with which the state government and many of its citizens clung to white supremacy, it would have been surprising had there been no violence. But Freedom Summer came. And the violence came.

Events in the years just before 1964 promised to threaten white supremacy in Mississippi, and thus help to explain why the white response to Freedom Summer was so vigorous and so visceral. Determined to thwart the 1954 *Brown* decision and other challenges to racial segregation, white Mississippians in the Delta created the Citizens' Council, a group that, according to one historian of the civil rights movement, "pursu[ed] the agenda of the Klan with the demeanor of the Rotary Club." The Mississippi legislature followed suit with the Sovereignty Commission, a state agency tasked with thwarting racial integration in the state and with rallying support for Jim Crow throughout the region.⁸ With the testing of segregated transportation and other facilities by civil rights activists and voter registration work in the early 1960s, white opposition to the civil rights movement in Mississippi gained renewed energy. In 1961 the Congress of Racial Equality (CORE) determined to assess the Interstate Commerce Commission's willingness to enforce the Supreme Court's 1960 ruling in *Bruce Boynton v. Virginia* that prohibited racial segregation in interstate terminal facilities and bus seating. White and black Freedom Riders took commercial buses from Virginia into the Deep South. Violence against the riders peaked in Anniston, Alabama, where Klansmen, with the cooperation of Alabama law enforcement officers, attempted to force an end to the Freedom Rides. A mob there firebombed a Greyhound bus; the riders barely escaped their attackers' plans to burn them alive inside the vehicle. A second bus, a Trailways, was boarded by eight Klansmen, who beat the riders, showing special violence toward whites.

On May 17, a second wave of reinforcement riders left Nashville for Birmingham. When they and subsequent riders reached Jackson, Mississippi, they were not assaulted by mobs, but rather were quickly arrested, eventually filling both the Jackson city and Hinds County jails; many riders were taken to Parchman, the state's penitentiary, where they were held under harsh, degrading conditions in one of the nation's most notorious prisons. The *Jackson Daily News* wrote: "The ridiculous conduct of the so-called 'freedom riders' up to this point leaves an open question whether they should be in jail, at the Whitfield Mental Hospital or the Jackson Zoo." However, the state's goal to intimidate the riders into abandoning their plans to work for civil rights in Mississippi did not succeed. Historian John Dittmer points out that "veterans of the freedom rides were among the shock troops of the Mississippi movement of the 1960s, fanning out across the state, organizing the dispossessed."[9]

In the meantime, each year in the early 1960s brought evidence that the Jim Crow settlement in Mississippi was under fresh assault: in 1961, the Freedom Rides and attempts at black voter registration in McComb; in 1962, the racial integration of Ole Miss by James Meredith and efforts at voter registration in the Mississippi Delta; in 1963, the Jackson movement against segregated public accommodations and the Freedom Vote to demonstrate black Mississippians' desire to exercise their constitutional rights; and in 1964, the Mississippi Summer Project and Congress's passage of the Civil Rights Act. Still, the murders of black Mississippians Herbert Lee and Medgar Evers, among many others, as well as the earlier slayings of Emmett Till and Lamar Smith, demonstrated to all Mississippians that there were men in the state who believed that the Mississippi way of life was worth killing for. Questioning the established order brought consequences for blacks and whites alike and demanded an unusual tenacity and determination to act upon one's beliefs.

This book features the photographs and writings of one person who followed his convictions, spoke and acted against Jim Crow, and paid—physically and emotionally—for those actions. The heart of this book is a group of forty-two black and white photographs taken by the Reverend R. Edwin King Jr. in the summer of 1964.[10] King, by that time long involved with civil rights activities, worked closely with the major civil rights efforts in the state during that year. Most notably, he was a leader in the formation of the Mississippi Freedom Democratic Party (MFDP) and served as a delegate to the Atlantic City Democratic convention that August when the MFDP challenged the seating of the state's all-white Democratic slate of delegates. He counseled and advised summer volunteers and leaders of the various civil rights organizations. He corresponded with and invited students and clergymen to participate in the Mississippi movement.

He also had the presence of mind sometimes to carry a camera. The bulk of the photographs in this book were taken by King in June and July of 1964 in Greenwood, Jackson, Philadelphia, and Madison County, Mississippi; a few were taken in Atlantic City, New Jersey. The content is exceptionally rich: Martin Luther King shooting pool in Philadelphia, and then exhorting a crowd of young black men to believe in themselves and to register to vote; Andrew Young and Martin Luther King interviewing victims of Klan violence in Philadelphia; King and Ralph Abernathy inspecting the ruins of the burned Mt. Zion Methodist Church; black and white volunteers in candid shots in the Council of Federated Organizations (COFO) office on Lynch Street in Jackson; and veteran movement activist Bob Moses in the Pratt Memorial Methodist Church in Jackson after listening to Martin Luther King speak on behalf of the Mississippi Freedom Democratic Party.

Photographs of civil rights activists and activities are not rare. Scholars have long noted that the civil rights movement of the 1950s and 1960s was to that point the most photographed and filmed social movement in American history. Of course, the media did more than document the movement. American and international press coverage of those events shaped observers' understandings of the significance of the history they were witnessing and figured in the ways both supporters and opponents of the movement conducted themselves.[11] For instance, one of the avowed purposes of Mississippi's Sovereignty Commission was to provide speakers, written material, and film to the rest of the nation to assure other Americans that all Mississippians were satisfied with the state's racial order.[12] State business and tourism interests were also concerned that national coverage of the civil rights movement was potentially bad

for business. Northern journalists too were well aware of that fact. One wrote:

> The state very much wants tourist business. Consequently, tourist information centers and guide books are very common, but they omit mention of some sights the more adventuresome or curious tourist might like to see. For example, they do not mention the Reverend R. Edwin King, a white native of Vicksburg who has an authentic Ku Klux Klan cross. He found it one morning in his front yard . . . The Reverend King, who is a Methodist minister and an integration leader, keeps the cross in his tool shed. There is no charge for viewing it.[13]

Movement participants as well documented their efforts, both as witness to the significance of their work and as visual evidence to convince observers throughout the nation that conditions in Mississippi were particularly un-American and demanded amelioration. The Student Nonviolent Coordinating Committee (SNCC) itself had an official photographer, Danny Lyon, from 1962 to 1964. In 1964 SNCC published *The Movement*, a documentary history of recent civil rights work in the South and in other parts of the nation. Along with scores of memoirs and autobiographies by civil rights activists, university and commercial presses have published collections of photographs by journalists who documented the social revolutions of the 1960s. And recently, the University Press of Mississippi published a collection of photographs taken by a number of movement activists themselves.[14]

However, this book is different in significant ways from all those others. First, King's status as a liberal white Mississippian active in the movement means that these photographs and words represent a rare perspective. Also, unlike many members of the state and national press, King was a trusted figure to the subjects he photographed. Consequently, the national figures and local people in the pages that follow appear candid and relaxed. The collection, then, might usefully be considered as family photos from the Freedom Summer movement. Each photograph is accompanied by Ed King's reflections on the specific photograph, the summer of 1964, or the civil rights movement in Mississippi in general. The combination of the unpublished photographs with King's unpublished writings makes the book a significant record—a firsthand account by one of the most important civil rights activists in Mississippi history. Some of the words in the pages here below are drawn from King's own unpublished memoir material, while much is taken as well from various oral histories conducted with King or interviews and correspondence that I have had with him in recent years. The words and photographs in the pages to follow, then, represent a candid perspective of Ed King's record and recollections of that significant summer, a perspective that especially deserves full acknowledgment by historians and other people interested in the history of the civil rights movement.

As we reach the fiftieth anniversary of so many significant moments in the civil rights movement in Mississippi, Rev. Edwin King deserves fresh recognition for his work on behalf of the state of Mississippi and its citizens, black and white. Many Mississippians had concluded by midcentury that the state was beyond redemption. King might well have joined and remained part of the migration that took so many Mississippians in search of a freer climate. Instead, believing that "there was no hope [of] the white community doing anything significant to change itself," in late 1962 King and his wife, Jeannette, both native white Mississippians, decided to return to Mississippi to participate in some way in the movement for social change spreading in the state.[15] They knew, as so many black Mississippians did, that such work carried the possibility of danger as well as ostracism from those who admired, feared, or simply acquiesced in the status quo. Their involvement in civil rights work would also cost the Kings and their families many old friendships. Indeed, King's interest in racial justice and reconciliation had already by that time caused enough controversy to force his parents to leave the state. A fellow Methodist minister told the Kings: "I want to tell you something very important, and I hope this makes you feel better. I do not for a minute believe that you are communists. I have listened to some of the people who say you are, and I don't accept their arguments. However, I'm afraid your son is."[16] Such rhetoric demonstrates the powerful confluence of anti-Communist and anti–civil rights attitudes in the state—as well as the nation—at the time, and helps to explain why so many white Mississippians saw the questioning of the Jim Crow order as radicalism that was at least irresponsibility, if not much worse.[17] Such attitudes produced an atmosphere of great potential peril for Ed King and other civil rights activists in the early 1960s.

Over time, King became "the most visible white activist in the Mississippi movement," according to historian John Dittmer, who notes that King "was ostracized by his family, scorned by his colleagues in the clergy, and later shunned by 'New South' white moderates who entered the political arena only after it was safe to do so."[18] Ed King bore witness to his faith and took a stand for basic civil rights for black Mississippians; the words and images in this book explore and document that stand. Given Mississippi's well-earned overall reputation for "official tyranny," as a SNCC document characterized it, King's active dissent from racial orthodoxy becomes all the more remarkable.[19]

By itself, King's liberalism did not make him unique. There were a number of white Mississippians who by 1960 or so felt that "something was wrong" in the state, and that white Mississippians could not realistically maintain the prevailing racial order forever. However, most of these dissenters in thought kept their own counsel, hesitating to speak out because of the implicit threats or other dangers risked by white Mississippians who seemed to question the racial status quo in a state that seemed to become less tolerant of dissent each year in the late 1950s and early 1960s. Those who did attack the system, such as University of Mississippi history professor James Silver, whose head was routinely called for by newspaper editorialists and state legislators after he published *Mississippi: The Closed Society* (1964), offered cautionary examples of the prudence of silence. In McComb, the previously well-respected family of Red and Malva Heffner was bullied out of town after daring even to speak to civil rights workers.

That said, a handful of journalists did call for fairness and obedience to the law. Sidna Brower, editor of the *Mississippian*, the Ole Miss student newspaper, counseled calm in the wake of campus riots over the admission of James Meredith. For that act, she received national praise, but also the scorn of many fellow students. Longtime Mississippi newspaper editor Hodding Carter Jr. was a voice of moderation with the Greenville *Delta Democrat-Times*. P. D. East, editor of *The Petal Paper*, enjoyed tweaking the Citizens' Coun-cil and other supporters of white supremacy. Ed King, in fact, sold subscriptions to *The Petal Paper* to fellow progressive students and teachers at Millsaps College. Hazel Brannon Smith won a Pulitzer Prize for her denunciations of white supremacy in the *Lexington Advertiser*. Smith became a close friend and advisor to the Kings. And Philadelphia, Mississippi, resident Florence Mars also deserves recognition for her denunciation of violence in Neshoba County.[20] Such voices were certainly the exception, though, and no other white Mississippian so consistently put himself on the line in the 1960s for liberal, Christian principles as did Ed King.

This collection of photographs and writings represents a coherent narrative not simply because of the photographer and the time, but also because of the story that they collectively tell of a moment of hope and anticipation. Ed King believed in and still believes in a vision of Christian community in which racial divisions and misunderstandings have been reconciled, the "beloved community" anticipated by Martin Luther King Jr. and SNCC in its early years. In the pages that follow, King refers to the end of the summer of 1964 as "the last days of the movement," a characterization that seems puzzling given the significant events of the ensuing years. What did seem to end following the year 1964, however, was a basic agreement among civil rights organizations and activists that had permeated the movement since Martin Luther King Jr. gained national prominence. Before the end of 1964, it was relatively easy for white activists to maintain that the major voices and much grassroots opinion within the civil rights movement held that nonviolent protest was the best strategy to achieve their goals, that a coalition of black and white activists should work together, and that racial integration was one of the chief ends of the freedom struggle. The years after 1964 witnessed the growth of a black nationalism and separatism that rejected those aims. In retrospect, the tensions within the movement that led to stresses and eventual breakdown in the multiracial coalition seem clear. But to the movement people and summer volunteers pictured and described in this book, the disillusionment was yet to come.

These photographs, then, represent a time when most summer volunteers and other movement workers believed that their efforts in Mississippi during those months in 1964 and later could bear fruit and that the system might still work. After 1964, that belief was harder for many people, especially many veterans of Freedom Summer, to maintain. In Mississippi and elsewhere in the nation, the alliances that constituted the COFO working arrangement shortly began to unravel. While it would be a mistake to characterize the summer of 1964 as a simpler time than the years that followed, the words and photographs of Ed King in the pages that follow do represent a period of hope, great ambition, momentum, and serious sense of purpose and possibility within the civil rights movement in Mississippi.

R. Edwin King Jr. is a native Mississippian, born in Vicksburg in 1936 to Ralph and Julia King and educated in the public schools there. His mother's family had deep roots in the state, with a Revolutionary War veteran ancestor's widow lying in Mississippi soil. His grandfather, J. W. Tucker, was sheriff of Warren County and had a bust of Robert E. Lee in his antebellum living room; his great-grandfather had fought with General Lee in Virginia. King's father and his family, on the other hand, had no longstanding Mississippi

connections; they came instead from West Virginia and the Oklahoma Territory before his father settled in Louisiana.[21] Nothing, however, in either family's history foreshadowed the fundamental challenge to the state's racial status quo that Ed King would embrace in the late 1950s and 1960s. Indeed, all evidence suggests that King's family were viewed by their neighbors and fellow Methodists as solid, middle-class southerners with no troubling political views. And Ed King himself makes no claims to a precocious radicalism. In high school, in fact, he won an American history award sponsored by the Daughters of the American Revolution.[22] Most young men from King's background found it simple to presume that the Mississippi way of life was solid and that it offered predictable rewards to those who gained an education, went to work, and played by the rules. It would have been easy, then, for King, as for many white Mississippians, not to have given much thought to the Jim Crow society that operated around him, especially any kind of thought leading to a conviction that it needed to be or could be changed.

King's early years sound much like those of many other white Mississippians who came of age in the 1940s and 1950s, and later spoke or wrote of those years, including the great Mississippi memoirist, Willie Morris. King has written of his childhood in words strikingly similar to Lillian Smith's in her memoir of a Georgia childhood of an earlier generation, *Killers of the Dream* (1949):

> All Mississippians were taught the racial facts of life early. I was no exception. The patterns of segregation were so absolute and so assumed that there was no need for explicit teaching . . . My parents . . . taught me and my younger brother, Mack . . . to respect

myself and other people, to respect family, church, society, state and nation. No teachings were overtly racist. White superiority was taken for granted. Middle class children were taught a few specific things—such as not to use the word "nigger" and not to hate.[23]

What, then, caused King to question the racial segregation that he and most other white Mississippians grew up accepting as the established order of things? For one thing, King was old enough to have grown up before the poisonous post-*Brown* decision atmosphere, in which the defense of the "Mississippi way of life" became increasingly strident. King recalled that he "happened to be there at a moment when you could still ask questions about race in Mississippi."[24] King also credits his membership in the Methodist Church for introducing him to broader national conversations about social issues and the responsibility of the Christian church. "I was proud of the national connections of the Methodist Church in Mississippi, something I began to understand when in high school. I soon became aware of strong liberal statements of the national church favoring integration (and the contradictions of the actual practice of segregation in the church)."[25] That connection to a national church proved fateful; it was a connection that provided access to points of view that the state's Southern Baptists, for example, among some other denominations, did not hear. King did have some school friends as well in the Episcopal Church who were also opened by national denominational conversations to questions on segregation. But those voices and that openness to questions were increasingly silenced in Mississippi by the 1960s.

An awakening to conditions in King's hometown of Vicksburg also led him to question what most white Mississippians took to be the "racial facts of life," as King referred to them. Like many middle-class and upper-class whites, King was accustomed to a kind of noblesse oblige attitude toward black Mississippians, a practice that manifested itself in occasional donations of used clothing or holiday gift baskets of food or a comfortable paternalism that allowed many whites to believe that their duties—as Christians or otherwise—toward their black neighbors had been satisfied. However, a natural disaster in Vicksburg served to shake King's conception of race relations as well as the fundamental conditions of black life in the city. In 1953 a tornado struck Vicksburg, causing colossal damage to property as well as loss of life. King and other high school friends volunteered during the city's relief efforts, working for the Red Cross and other agencies. King later reflected that working in the black section of town (a principle of separation that itself seemed without question) allowed him for the first time to see "the terrible poverty and living conditions of many black residents of Vicksburg . . . I was not the only student to realize this was partially the result of segregation, that there was no such thing as separate but equal. Before this I had been blind."[26] King had learned how little he, like most other white Mississippians, really had known about his black neighbors, a lesson fundamentally at odds with the white southern tenet that blacks and whites knew each other well.

King's college years occurred in a time and place that constituted one of the few venues in Mississippi where a person could hear, if he wished, relatively open discussion of the prevailing social order. After graduating from Vicksburg's Carr Central High School in 1954, that fall King entered Jackson's Millsaps

College, an institution affiliated with the Methodist Church. There, King studied sociology and continued to ask searching questions about race relations and the demands of Christian faith in Mississippi. Historian Charles Marsh has noted that some faculty and students at Millsaps participated in the Intercollegiate Fellowship, an interracial discussion group that included participants from the University of Mississippi, Mississippi State University, Jackson College, and Tougaloo College.[27] Jeannette Sylvester, who would marry King, was from Jackson. She was also a Methodist who earned degrees from Millsaps College and the Boston University School of Social Work. She wrote of those Intercollegiate Fellowship meetings: "It was the first chance I had as a white Mississippian to meet in the same room with black people and discuss personal and intellectual issues. In a short space of time, these meetings accomplished what all the religious (do unto others) and social (be kind to everyone) ideas had just talked about."[28] Such spaces for interracial dialogue became rarer in the state in the late 1950s and early 1960s. It was easy for white Mississippians literally to have no idea of black ideas or aspirations.

While Millsaps was by the late 1950s developing a reputation in the state for progressive (or potentially dangerous) thinking on matters of race and race relations, it is important not to exaggerate the degree of liberalism prevailing at the college. Still, unlike the University of Mississippi and other state-funded institutions, Millsaps College administrators and faculty enjoyed relatively less legislative scrutiny of campus speakers and other signs of the questioning of official mores. The fact that some students and faculty were willing, however cautiously, even to discuss race relations invited public attention and scorn and

worried college administrators. The Jackson newspapers, the Citizens' Council, and concerned alumni and Methodist laypeople did in fact keep an eye on the Jackson campus. Such was the climate in Mississippi in those years.

An important influence on King, during his Millsaps years and later, was Tougaloo sociology professor Ernst Borinski. A refugee from Nazi Germany, Borinski held what were to most white Mississippians radical views on race relations. He provided important leadership for the Intercollegiate Fellowship and taught an informal, interracial Russian language class in the Millsaps College library. Borinski's remark at a Millsaps forum that "racial segregation violates Christian principles" caused scandal. The Citizens' Council had become a powerful organization in the state, and the interest of Millsaps students in interracial dialogue attracted their attention. The Jackson council chapter president charged that the college appeared "to be in the apparent position of undermining everything we are fighting for." Millsaps responded with a statement affirming the college's commitment to segregation. Another important influence on King was native Mississippian and chair of the sociology department George Maddox, a critic of Jim Crow in Mississippi. King remembers: "He was very involved in Millsaps-Tougaloo cooperative programs and close to Dr. Ernst Borinski. Maddox felt Mississippi was hopeless and doomed; he left [in 1959] almost as much a refugee as Borinski had left Germany."[29] The critical attention attracted by these dissenters and its consequences could not have been lost on King and other Millsaps College students.

When the summer of 1964 began, Ed King had been involved with civil rights work for several years. His formal and informal education broadened his interest in and experience with the emerging civil rights movement. After graduating from Millsaps in 1958, King began studies at the Boston University School of Theology, where Robert Bergmark and George Maddox, some of the Millsaps faculty whose liberalism had most influenced him, had also studied. King earned a master of divinity degree (1961) and a master of theology degree (1963). His deepening interest in racial justice and reconciliation fit well with the commitments and scholarship of the school's faculty.[30] Ed King first met Dr. Martin Luther King Jr. in Montgomery, Alabama, in December 1958, in a meeting arranged through the Boston University School of Theology. In March 1960, he was first arrested in a sit-in in Montgomery, Alabama, where he had gone from Boston on behalf of the Fellowship of Reconciliation to seek white liberals willing to talk and work with local blacks. At that time still hoping to keep a low profile in order to secure a church in Mississippi, King was arrested while eating in a black-owned restaurant with Rev. Ralph Abernathy in a police raid targeting the Southern Christian Leadership Conference, led by Martin Luther King Jr. and Abernathy. His second arrest—deliberately sought this time in a legal strategy designed by SCLC attorney Fred Gray—followed when he invited a black Methodist clergyman, Rev. Elroy Embry, to dine with him in the Plantation Dining Room of the Jefferson Davis Hotel, where King had registered as a guest.[31] The two ministers were subsequently convicted of disorderly conduct and trespassing on private property. They served a week's sentence in black and white striped outfits on a convict work gang. King's growing involvement in civil rights activities ultimately caused his alienation from the Christian denomination he hoped to serve.

In June 1963, King was refused membership in the all-white Mississippi Conference of Methodists; he later joined the Central Jurisdiction, the conference of black Methodists; he was the only white member. This affiliation would be fateful for King, who subsequently became a spiritual and strategic counselor to the civil rights movement in the state, as well as chaplain at historically black Tougaloo College.

During the fall of 1962, Ed and Jeannette King followed the alarming story of the integration of Ole Miss from Massachusetts. They began seriously to consider returning to the state. We "had wanted to be here [in Mississippi]," said King, "not in the movement's sense, but to be with white Mississippi during that kind of crisis." But King already determined that he wished to take some active role in the grassroots civil rights movement unfolding in the state.[32] "My wife, Jeannette, and I experienced the Civil Rights Movement of the 1950s and 1960s from unique perspectives—participant/observers and part of the people who would have to live with the changes."[33] Tougaloo sociologist Ernst Borinski informed King that the chaplaincy at Tougaloo College was open and urged King to consider the position. Charles Marsh writes: "For his part, Medgar Evers, who had become the NAACP field secretary for Mississippi, told King point blank that he should return; in fact, he must return to fill the vacancy of the chaplaincy at Tougaloo College. King recalls Evers' words: 'You have to come back because we need you, because this, my friend, is your calling.'"[34] King's decision to come to Tougaloo would profoundly shape his life—not only in 1963 and 1964, but also in the decades that followed. No professional decision that he made would prove more consequential.

In 1963, Methodist Bishop Marvin Franklin approved King's appointment as Tougaloo College's chaplain. The college is located just north of Jackson, the state capital. King would remain chaplain at Tougaloo until 1967. King says: "I heard [that Bishop Franklin] bragged about my appointment when he was being attacked as so many of the young ministers in the state were losing their pulpits and being driven out of state . . . He bragged that he had one minister working at a black college."[35] Tougaloo had become a relative hotbed of civil rights activity when the Kings arrived at the end of January. To be more precise, Tougaloo students and a few professors, such as John Salter and Ernst Borinski, were beginning to test the possibilities of breaching the state's Jim Crow laws and customs. However, many of Tougaloo's professors viewed direct action campaigns with the same worry that other middle-class black Mississippians did. While Tougaloo was a private institution, the state of Mississippi did have ways of threatening the college, as Ed King, Tougaloo's President A. Daniel Beittel, and others would learn. The Mississippi state legislature did have the authority to revoke the college's charter, a threat they soon held over the head of the administration. In 1964, the Sovereignty Commission would suggest to Tougaloo College that if Ed King and President Beittel were fired, then the state legislature would not be forced to revoke the charter of a school that the lieutenant governor characterized as "a haven of 'queers, quirks, political agitators and possibly some communists.'" There was also pressure to remove Professor John Salter, but he had by that time voluntarily left for full-time work in the civil rights movement. Ed King stood fast and resisted pressure to leave, although he became the subject of increasing scrutiny and threats to his safety.

In 1964 Beittel was forced from the Tougaloo presidency under circumstances that never received a full public airing, a cautionary reminder of the length of the state's reach.[36] Ed King maintains that Tougaloo College was rewarded for its caution with the money and approval of the New York philanthropic foundation world and that the Sovereignty Commission by itself did not arrange the pressure on and incentives toward the school. King writes, "I believe that there were deep federal fingers influencing the naïve Sovereignty Commission to be the patsy." Historian John Dittmer notes that in 1963 Brown University had launched a cooperative program with Tougaloo. The president of Brown, Barnaby Keeney, did not approve of "Tougaloo's active involvement in the black struggle." Tougaloo president Beittel received news from the United Church of Christ, Tougaloo's sponsor, that he was fired from the presidency and would need to vacate his office at the end of the spring term. While Beittel was assured that there was no collusion between Brown University and the Ford Foundation, which had promised funding for the cooperative venture, "Keeney's private correspondence, however, substantiates Beittel's accusations" that there certainly was. Beittel was indeed removed, and the Ford Foundation subsequently granted money to Brown University. Whatever the nature of Brown University's involvement with Tougaloo, the college's students were not silenced. Civil rights activity on campus did decline, but never totally. And if there was a strategic and intellectual heart of the civil rights movement in Mississippi from 1961 through 1964, Tougaloo College was it.[37]

In 1963, Tougaloo students had been instrumental in the Capitol Street business boycott, designed to force Jackson merchants into treating black customers with fairness and dignity. They had also initiated a sit-in campaign on March 27, 1961, when nine Tougaloo students took seats in the whites-only Jackson Municipal Library and began reading. The Tougaloo Nine, as they became known, were arrested, charged with breach of peace, fined, and given suspended sentences. And in 1963 Tougaloo students also provided the civil rights movement with one of its most striking, iconic images. The direct action campaign was planned by the Jackson movement strategy committee and its chairman, John Salter, under the overall leadership of Medgar Evers of the NAACP. Students challenged a Jim Crow custom in a state that had tenaciously denied even token accommodation of black demands for civil rights. Ed King recalled: "In an act designed to defy white Mississippi and inspire black Mississippi, they would sit together and break bread together, should they be served, at the lunch counter of Woolworth's in Jackson."[38] Three Tougaloo students willing to risk arrest volunteered for this action: Memphis Norman from Wiggins, Pearlina Lewis from Jackson, and Anne Moody from Centreville.[39] The students were seated, but were ignored by the waitresses after they were told to move to another counter, where blacks were served. A white crowd slowly gathered, especially after noon, when students from a nearby white high school began to enter the store. Police on Capitol Street observed the scene but took no action inside the store, as the mob began to beat and kick the Tougaloo students, several of whom were knocked or dragged from the lunch counter stools. The police arrested only picketers outside (including Jeannette King and Margrit Garner, both of Tougaloo) carrying signs that read, "Jackson Needs a Bi-Racial Committee," a call for a venue where black Jacksonians could present their grievances to white Jacksonians.[40]

The mob was particularly incensed by the presence at the counter of white student Joan Trumpauer, or "the white nigger," as one referred to her. Trumpauer, a native of Arlington, Virginia, had transferred to Tougaloo from Duke University. She had been one of the CORE Freedom Riders arrested in 1961 and jailed at Parchman, the state penitentiary. Concerned about the conditions under which she was being held, her mother wrote to Fred Smith, the penitentiary superintendent. His reply reveals the sexual as well as racial taboos the civil rights workers were widely believed by white Mississippians to flout: "What I can't understand is why as a mother you permitted a minor white girl to gang up with a bunch of negro bucks and white hoodlums to ramble over this country with the express purpose of violating the laws of certain states and attempting to invite acts of violence."[41] Just before the Freedom Rides, the *Jackson Daily News* had issued a taunting invitation to the "restless race mixers" to spend the summer at Parchman and "have a real 'vacation' on a real plantation."[42]

Native Mississippian Anne Moody, one of the other students at the counter, remembered the scene in Woolworth's:

> There were now four of us, two whites and two Negroes, all women. The mob started smearing us with ketchup, mustard, sugar, pies, and everything on the counter. Soon Joan and I were joined by John Salter, but the moment he sat down he was hit on the jaw with what appeared to be brass knuckles. Blood gushed from his face and someone poured salt into the open wound. Ed King, Tougaloo's chaplain, rushed to him.

The mob beat and taunted the student protesters for nearly three hours in front of television cameras. Jackson police did nothing to stop the violence. Eventually, the Woolworth's manager closed the store in an attempt to bring the protest and the violence to an end.

By this time, Tougaloo's president, Dr. A. Daniel Beittel, had learned of the sit-in and the violence via a telephone call from Ed King and had arrived on the scene. According to Anne Moody, Beittel insisted that the ninety police outside the store protect the students from further violence. "When we got outside," she wrote, "they formed a single line that blocked the mob from us. However, they were allowed to throw at us everything they had collected . . . After the sit-in, all I could think of was how sick Mississippi whites were." Ed King adds: "The event shocked sensitive people in the nation, but was shown to Mississippi TV audiences only in censored versions . . . The incident is indicative of the soul of the Movement and the almost lack of soul bred by the racism and fascism of the state of Mississippi."[43] Of the photographs of the Woolworth's sit-in taken by Fred Blackwell, historian M. J. O'Brien writes: "Every major civil rights museum has [one] hanging somewhere within its displays." Native Mississippian Blackwell recalled of the images: "It hit me when I was photographing that they were right and we were wrong."[44]

Along with Tougaloo colleague John Salter, King also tested the segregation of public events at his alma mater, Methodist-affiliated Millsaps College. King and Salter began taking groups of Tougaloo students to music concerts and theater productions at the ironically named Christian Center, where they were turned away and threatened with the police. John Salter wrote to Millsaps president Dr. Ellis Finger that the treatment he

and the Tougaloo students received was consistent with "neither genuine Christianity, nor functional democracy, nor academic health." In a subsequent letter, Salter warned Finger that he and Tougaloo students "shall return to your College many times indeed in the future." When Ed and Jeannette King brought an integrated group to the Christian Center, Dean John Christmas informed them that the college did not admit Negroes to Millsaps events and threatened to call the police if they did not leave. Theater director Lance Goss attempted to force the group from the theater by insisting that they take money from him as a refund for their prepurchased tickets, which had been bought by sympathetic Millsaps teachers and students, then given to their Tougaloo friends. Soon seven police cars arrived with howling police dogs. The Tougaloo people made their exit from the theater by a side door. King protested: "That Millsaps College, a Christian, liberal arts college, would go to the point of calling the Jackson police with their famous dogs to leave the Christian Center building is hard to believe."[45] Tougaloo College president Dr. Dan Beittel joined King and Salter in negotiations with Millsaps administrators, who then agreed to open all such public events to all of the public. While King's work, then, had borne fruit, it had also made him increasingly notorious to white segregationists and vulnerable to retaliation.

In 1963 and 1964 King also led students, fellow ministers, and other civil rights workers in a campaign to integrate Jackson's racially segregated churches and thus promote discussion by the silent moderates about matters of conscience, religious teaching and racism. Those "pray-ins" and the subsequent frequent arrests made King a highly visible enemy and target of the "closed society" that prevailed in Mississippi in those years. The white Protestant churches, home of a great majority of the state's white worshippers, were largely officially silent on the question of segregation, a legacy that some denominations and some churches have failed fully to acknowledge to this day. When some churches, such as Galloway Methodist Church in Jackson, were challenged to open their doors to worshippers of all races, many members of the congregation showed their support of the old way of life by pushing back, openly denouncing calls for integrated worship. Ed King recalled: "Dr. W. B. Selah, pastor of Galloway Methodist Church, resigned his pulpit once blacks brought to the Sunday morning worship by Medgar Evers were denied admission."[46] Despite such setbacks, King saw reasons to be optimistic. He wrote to a midwestern supporter: "The church visits seem to have made a real impression. Our students have been invited to join two churches and are welcome at a few others. Actions of national denominations give us hope for most of the others." Anne Moody remembered that a Jackson Episcopal church offered her and other African American Tougaloo students a sincere welcome: "When the services were over the minister invited us to visit again. He said it as if he meant it, and I began to have a little hope."[47]

Ed King was of course not the only white Mississippi clergyman who saw the contradictions that a Jim Crow society presented to the tenets of his faith. In Oxford, Rev. Duncan Gray Jr. called for justice and obedience to the law from St. Peter's Episcopal Church and on the Ole Miss campus in the fall of 1962 during the riots occasioned by James Meredith's integration of the university. Still, many Mississippi Christians, both clergy and laity, apparently agreed with the sentiments

of Rev. Eldie Hicks, pastor of the First Baptist Church of Waynesville, who wrote in 1964: "I am personally convinced that what is going on here involves more than the civil rights issue, and that it is sinister and dangerous beyond anything we have yet supposed."[48] Most Mississippi residents, then and for years to come, accepted segregated worship services as one of the racial facts of life. Half a century later, memories of those years remain raw. One scholar who studied the church integration initiative contacted Jackson churches asking their assistance. He found that "most of the churches ignored my request or declined to assist me ... one church denied ever having turned away anyone on the basis of race."[49] Such recent intransigence suggests perhaps some of the depth of resistance that King and the other civil rights workers faced in those earlier years.

The year 1963 was pivotal for Ed King and for the Jackson movement. John Salter, Medgar Evers, Ed King, and Tougaloo students continued direct action nonviolent protests aimed at integrating Jackson businesses and other institutions. Jackson mayor Allen Thompson responded to the pressure by adding large numbers of men to the police force. "Everything intensified in May 1963," wrote King. "Within weeks more than 1,000 people, mostly children and college students, had been jailed in non-violent demonstrations and held in newly prepared 'concentration camp–like' facilities in the animal pens and exhibit buildings of the Mississippi State Fairgrounds."[50] To add insult to the experience, the Jackson police transported many of the arrested protestors in garbage trucks.

Then on June 12, 1963, Medgar Evers, probably the best-known face of black protest in Mississippi, was assassinated. Shortly after midnight, Evers returned home after a civil rights rally at Jackson's New Jerusalem Baptist Church. Evers carried a stack of "Jim Crow Must Go" t-shirts up his driveway, which was not lighted to make his home-comings less conspicuous. He was shot in the back, and died from his injuries on the way to the hospital. His accused assassin, Byron De La Beckwith, was not convicted of the crime until 1994. After Evers's June 15 funeral at Jackson's Masonic Temple, at-tended by thousands of mourners, some five thousand people took to the Jackson streets as part of the funeral procession, which be-came a nonviolent protest, where tempers eventually flared as the mournful celebration of Evers's life became a demonstration. Many protestors, among them Ed King, were beat-en and arrested by Jackson police.[51] Ed King described his arrest and detention at the fair-grounds that day:

> The man standing next to me was a stranger . . . He had been badly beaten by the police. On the back of his head was an ugly patch of blood, almost black. . . . Flecks of bright, fresh blood oozed out of the head wound . . . flies even crawled in his hair and in the wound on his scalp . . . I found what little courage I still had, and slowly turned my head in his direction as we whispered, hoping the police would not notice . . . I . . . pulled a handker-chief from my pocket, and stepped over to the wounded man. An officer ran up and shouted to us. "Hey, King, what the hell you doing out of line?" . . . He raised his rifle in the air, hold-ing the butt end ready. "You nigger-loving son of a bitch . . . You touch his head, and you get one just like it" . . . I was afraid . . . If the man was dying at my feet, I would not look down. There was no courage, no goodness, no decency left, only fear. I spoke to the police-man, "I understand what you can do."[52]

Three days later, Ed King and John Salter were involved in a serious automobile wreck in Jackson that shattered King's jaw and near-ly killed him. John Salter writes:

> Some yards ahead of us, lunging out of a side-street to our left and past a stop sign, came a car driven by a white youth in such a fashion that another car coming down toward us in the other lane was forced, by the white youth's car, into our lane, approaching us head on while the white youth quickly manipulated his car over to the side . . . The youth's father, a former public official, was one of Jackson's most prominent Citizens Council members.

With Evers dead, and with King and Salter hospitalized, the Jackson movement lost the opportunity to see how far they and the Tougaloo students could have pushed Jack-son and what fruit that might have borne for civil rights work in other parts of the state. The suspicious automobile accident and Evers's assassination served to break the Jack-son movement just as Evers, a loose cannon in the eyes of the national NAACP, seemed poised to force real change rather than token-ism upon Mississippi.[53] In Ed King's judg-ment, the national government, especially self-described liberals, are particular villains here. The Kennedy administration, he main-tains, feared an alliance of Evers with Mar-tin Luther King, and was more interested in reelection plans than in justice for black Americans. Evers, he believes, had the capac-ity to lead a strong people's movement, which might have unfolded in ways that threatened those people in Washington and throughout the United States who claimed to support civ-il rights in Mississippi, but who were instead primarily concerned with overseeing the na-ture and pace of social change.

Despite his injuries, which required numerous surgeries through the subsequent years, King was also deeply involved in 1963 in the organization of what became the Mississippi Freedom Democratic Party. The MFDP was at once an education in grassroots civics for black Mississippians and a statement to the rest of the nation that black Mississippians were in fact deeply interested in politics, the denial of which had been a staple of white rhetoric since the overthrow of Reconstruction. Historians have long noted that there was a stubborn tradition of black voting in various parts of the state. And black Mississippians also recalled times during which black Mississippians not only voted, but also held office. Holmes County's Robert Clark, who in 1967 became the first black Mississippian elected to the state legislature in the twentieth century, recalled a grandfather who had been sheriff in the 1870s before being run out of the county by Klan violence. A historian of the MFDP notes that Clark's story was "repeated over and over again by older black Mississippians and the younger Freedom Party organizers who met them."[54]

Eventually the MFDP would challenge the seating of the all-white Mississippi delegation at the 1964 Atlantic City Democratic presidential convention, where Mrs. Fannie Lou Hamer introduced a shocked national audience to revelations of violence against and intimidation of black voters.[55] Ed King has long held that the MFDP's eventual disappointment in their attempt to be seated instead of the regular Democratic delegation offers valuable insights into the perfidy of white liberal Democrats. The story of the development of the MFDP is complex. As with white politics in Mississippi, there were factions within black politics as well, ones that were often mostly personal. Those factions did not

cleave neatly along planes of social class or of age. It would not be accurate to describe the MFPD as the people's party and the NAACP as the home of the black middle class. The MFDP did in fact draw heavy support from poor blacks, especially in the Delta, but many members and leaders of the party, such as Aaron Henry and Ed King, were certainly of the middle class. It is accurate to say that not all black Mississippians were convinced of the wisdom of the Freedom Vote or of the Freedom Party. Some longtime NAACP activists, for example, were galled that the MFDP did not turn to them for leadership. Such an attitude is perhaps understandable, given the years of tireless, often seemingly thankless, work before 1964 by such NAACP stalwarts as Amzie Moore, E. W. Steptoe, and Aaron Henry himself.

As an indicator of black interest in voting, if nothing else, the results of the Freedom Vote are telling. In the fall of 1963, over eighty-three thousand black Mississippians cast their ballots in the Freedom Vote in what was for many of them their first participation in politics. They voted in churches and in black-owned businesses such as barbershops, beauty salons, bars, and gas stations. Ed King was the party's candidate for lieutenant governor, while pharmacist and longtime NAACP activist Aaron Henry of Clarksdale was the candidate for governor. Registered black voters were also asked to participate. Historian Charles Payne writes: "Those who were registered—fewer than twenty-five thousand Negroes statewide—were encouraged to vote in the regular election and write in the name of the Freedom candidates."[56] Henry and King campaigned on a platform that proposed radical changes to the status quo. Henry called for the abolition of segregation in all state and public facilities, the end of state funding for the Citizens' Council, the abolition of the Sovereignty Commission, a thorough integration of state and local police forces, the end of the prohibition of alcohol in the state, and civil service reform. In short, they called for a thorough transformation of Mississippi.[57] Many years later, King joked: "We lost on the Freedom Vote, and it was because we were both from the Delta. I was from the bottom of the Delta in Vicksburg, and he was from Clarksdale, and we figured there wasn't anything else unusual about our ticket." King's later joking aside, movement organizers considered the vote a success and a step toward greater achievements. David Dennis of CORE said that it "did much more for the movement, toward uniting Mississippi, than anything else we have done." John Dittmer notes: "Perhaps what was most remarkable was that neither Henry nor King were assaulted, a unique experience for both men."[58]

In 1964, Aaron Henry, Ed King, and many other civil rights workers built on the Freedom Vote to put together what became the Mississippi Freedom Democratic Party. The obstacles to black voting in the state were well-known and deliberately enforced. To vote, one had to pay a poll tax and pass a literacy test to the satisfaction of a county registrar of voters, "whose discretionary powers are enormous," noted activist Tom Hayden in 1964. As black attempts at registration grew more determined, white Mississippians responded with overt violence, as the murders of Herbert Lee and Louis Allen in Liberty attest, and with not so subtle invitations to violence, such as the publication of black registrants' names in local newspapers. Any challenge to the prevailing system of disfranchisement, then, was rightly perceived by most whites as a threat to the Jim Crow order.

In the face of the potential risks occasioned by these challenges, the MFDP and other activists anticipated the summer registration campaign. "The danger now is greater than it ever has been," noted an MFDP publication that summer, "and so is our hope."[59] But while some black Mississippians persevered and registered to vote throughout the state, by the mid-1960s Mississippi had the lowest percentage of black voters in the South and of course in the nation. While approximately 40 percent of eligible black voters were registered throughout the region, only 6 percent of black Mississippians were registered. Nine of the state's eighty-two counties had no registered black voters, with another twenty-five counties having less than 1 percent of the eligible black population registered.[60] The Mississippi Project in the summer of 1964 aimed to raise that percentage.

The activities of Freedom Summer should be placed within the broader context of the attempts at voter registration and other civil rights work that had been undertaken in the state since 1961. The Mississippi Project was an outgrowth of the movement activity that began in 1960 with the formation of the Student Nonviolent Coordinating Committee. SNCC, encouraged and counseled by longtime civil rights activist Ella Baker, organized students to participate in voter registration, sit-ins, and other direct nonviolent protest of Jim Crow in the South. SNCC also participated in the 1961 Freedom Rides. Plans, certainly the experiences to make those plans, for the 1964 "invasion" of Mississippi, then, might be said to stretch back several years. "SNCC," wrote Tom Hayden in 1964, "in its attempt to ignite a mass non-violent movement, designated the formidable and sovereign state of Mississippi as the site of its pilot project." The organization determined to register voters in McComb, Mississippi, in 1961. A railroad town in the southwestern part of the state, McComb, a city with a population of twelve thousand, reacted violently to the SNCC campaign and rebuffed their efforts so strongly that there were no outside attempts to organize in the town for three more years. However, argues historian Charles Payne, "McComb is always remembered as a defeat for SNCC, which is true in a narrow sense, but it overlooks the fact that SNCC learned in McComb that merely the process of organizing a town would attract young people, a few of whom were willing to identify completely with the organization's work."[61] One lesson that McComb taught SNCC's Mississippi Field Secretary Robert Moses, active in civil rights work in the state since 1961, was that the various groups acting in the state would have a greater likelihood of success were they to work together.[62] SNCC activity in McComb also drew upon and galvanized a group of young local activists who would continue to shape the community in the late 1960s and beyond.

Thus, the civil rights campaign in Mississippi in 1964 was conducted under the auspices of COFO, the Council of Federated Organizations. COFO brought together the efforts of the Student Nonviolent Coordinating Committee (SNCC), the Southern Christian Leadership Conference (SCLC), the Congress of Racial Equality (CORE), and local members of the National Association for the Advancement of Colored People (NAACP). The national NAACP was deeply ambivalent—at times seemingly hostile—towards the direct action campaigns that swept the South in the early 1960s, preferring to rely instead on its long tradition of litigation, a tradition with many victories to display, as the remedy for injustices.

Why Mississippi? One journalist wrote in 1964: "In taking on the toughest of the segregationist states, where Emmett Till, Mack Parker, and Medgar Evers died, there is widespread repetition of the slogan 'Crack Mississippi and you can crack the South.' It provides a rallying cry that expresses both the strategy of the project and its attractiveness to younger recruits in the civil rights movement."[63] "Mississippi is just a start," wrote one volunteer, "this whole country needs changing so that everyone can live a life in which he is able to realize his full capacities as a human being."[64] Why 1964? As a COFO memorandum explained, in words that stress both the significance and the difficulty of work in the state: "Mississippi at this juncture in the Movement has received too little attention."

> Either the civil rights struggle has to continue there as it has for the past few years, with small projects continuing to work in selected communities with no real progress on any fronts, or the Movement must concentrate on confronting Mississippi with a representative task force of such size as to force either the state and municipal governments to change their social and legal structure, or the Federal Government to intervene on behalf of the constitutional rights of its citizens.[65]

Not surprisingly, most white Mississippians were not prepared to greet the student volunteers as idealists with noble aims. The prospect of fundamental change to the state's "social and legal structure," as COFO put it, presented challenge enough to native Mississippians, let alone those people perceived as outside agitators. The terms in which many white Mississippians couched their distaste for the summer volunteers tells us much about the visceral level at which the movement struck them. A registrar of voters in Liberty told civil rights workers that "the Negro men were raping the white women up North, and that he didn't want and wouldn't allow such a thing to start down here in Mississippi." Newspapers and public officials rarely mentioned the summer volunteers without some critical reference to their appearance or their state of cleanliness. "If these wandering minstrels would simply go home, take a bath, shave and put on a clean pair of socks, then I know that Mississippi would be better off," said former governor Ross Barnett. "Why send a couple of carloads of marshals to look after them," he added, "when a case of Mister Clean would do a lot more good?"[66] A major state newspaper described them as "beatniks," "wild-eyed left wing nuts," and "unshaven and unwashed trash." Another opined that "the just plain stupid or ignorant or misled" were "meddling and muddling with things about which they know nothing and which concern them not."[67] The volunteers were of course motivated by a variety of reasons, among them idealism, a belief in the rule of law, and the desire to participate in a major social movement. Not all were necessarily motivated by utopian aims. Barney Frank, Harvard student and future congressman, said: "As conditions improve—and they will—the Negro will seek his spot in suburbia, drink his beer, and watch TV. That's fine! . . . I'm not here to build a perfect society, just to insure that the Negro gets a chance to live his life in his own way."[68] In the summer of 1964, though, Frank's assurance of black Mississippians' modest aims for middle-class consumerist comforts would not have soothed the anxieties of most white Mississippians.

Indeed, years of increasingly alarmist rhetoric had prepared many in the state to believe that the summer movement threatened the foundations of their culture. In a way, it did, of course; official white Mississippi prepared accordingly. For instance, Jackson's Mayor Allen Thompson, according to one magazine, "has been acting as though Armageddon were just around the corner." Thompson built up his police force—"twice as big as any city our size," he boasted, adding shotguns, tear gas, police dogs, and "the pride of Allen's Army," a twelve-man, thirteen-thousand-pound "battlewagon . . . abristle with shotguns, tear-gas guns, and a submachine gun." Thompson contended: "They are not bluffing and we are not bluffing. We're going to be ready for them . . . They won't have a chance."[69] Events later in the summer in Jackson and throughout the state showed that Thompson's threats reflected a potential for violence that existed throughout most of Mississippi.

Ed King was deeply involved with COFO and MFDP registration and organization efforts throughout the state in 1964. Although still a young man, he was in terms of length of service an elder statesman, certainly among white activists, and served as strategist and mentor to the college volunteers and other young workers in the state. Calling King "perhaps the most active political leader in the ranks of white radicals," a contemporary observer succinctly identified King's importance for the civil rights movement in Mississippi:

> During the summer of 1964, he took on some of the hardest jobs in the civil rights movement. King was, for example, one of the first people to go to the Southwest [the McComb area] to open the area for other workers who followed. He was also influential in organizing the Freedom Democrats . . . At great personal risk, King has taken the lead in forging a potentially influential party, representative of Negro aspirations.[70]

Photographer Matt Herron, who covered the civil rights movement for *Life*, *Look*, and *Time*, among other newsmagazines, remembered King as "the only white Mississippian who had joined the Civil Rights Movement outright (he was number one on the Klan's death list)."[71] Herron was not speaking figuratively. "The KKK circulated posters with photographs of the persons they targeted to kill."[72] The posters contained photos of Ed King, as well as Tougaloo students Anne Moody and Joan Trumpauer. The face of Mississippi NAACP Field Director Medgar Evers, assassinated in 1963, was marked over with an X. For King and other movement workers in the summer of 1964, then, the possibility of death was real and present, and black Mississippians certainly understood that the state was a place where some people could kill others with seeming impunity. The threat might come from a Klansman or a deputy sheriff, which in a number of cases turned out to be the same thing.

Before they reached Mississippi, some Mississippi Project volunteers might have underestimated what they faced in the Magnolia State. They had trained for one week in Oxford, Ohio, on the campus of the Western College for Women. Experienced volunteers explained the conditions under which black Mississippians lived and worked and what to expect from police, sheriffs, and other whites. Rev. Ed King conducted a memorial service in Ohio for Medgar Evers and explained Mississippi conditions to them, including the fact that because of biased television and press coverage, most white Mississippians had little informed notion of the civil rights movement in the state and of the level of white violence, official and unofficial, toward it. In Ohio, students preparing for Mississippi were tutored in the philosophy of nonviolence and received practical training in protecting one's head and genitals while being kicked and punched. Still, some volunteers had trouble taking Mississippi seriously. One night volunteers watched a CBS report on black voting in the state. "Some of the film," wrote one student, "was absolutely ridiculous—a big, fat, really fat and ugly white county registrar prevents Negroes from voting . . . Six of the staff members got up and walked out because it was so real to them while we laughed because it was so foreign to us."[73]

After trainees in Ohio learned that three civil rights workers were missing in eastern Mississippi, Mississippi became harder to laugh at.

Once they reached the state, student volunteers quickly learned from black Mississippians and other experienced volunteers of the risks their work entailed. Over time, no precaution seemed unnecessary. One volunteer wrote:

> It's night. It's hot. No lights because there aren't any curtains—meaning they can see you and you can't see them . . . You doze off and the phone rings again, about the fifth time, and the other end stays mum. By now you know that somebody, someone on the other side, knows where you are. Violence hangs overhead like dead air—it hangs there and maybe it will fall and maybe it won't . . . Something is in the air, something is going to happen, somewhere, sometime, to someone.[74]

The worry was not groundless, as the fates of the three missing workers in Philadelphia demonstrated.

The murders of James Chaney, Michael Schwerner, and Andrew Goodman in Philadelphia, Mississippi, on June 21, 1964, have become perhaps the one story most associated with Freedom Summer. Martin Luther King Jr. remarked of Philadelphia, "This town is the worst that I've seen. There is a complete reign of terror here."[75] The FBI missing persons poster is an iconic and commonly reproduced image of Freedom Summer. Mickey and Rita Schwerner were active, visible, and Jewish, all three characteristics that made them liable to retaliation from local whites. "In Meridian, Mike [*sic*] and Rita Schwerner, a young married couple from New York City, have transformed dingy second-floor doctors' offices into a pleasant five-room center with a 10,000-book library . . . [Their work appears] to be running smoothly."[76] No one—no one in Mississippi, at least—could have been surprised that there were people in the state willing to kill to preserve segregation. Ed King remembered: "We assumed that most of the leadership of the Movement would be dead by the end of the summer," which movement leadership believed to be the "last chance to do something against an already massive wave of violence." Stokely Carmichael and other movement leaders were at a meeting at Tougaloo College when they learned of the disappearance of the three men. No one was sent that evening to investigate because "we felt that anyone who came up here [to Neshoba County] would be killed . . . By morning we knew they were dead . . . we also said Goodman [who had been in the state less than one day] wouldn't understand . . . we would even have said that Goodman is too American to understand why they're going to kill him." Predictably, a number of Mississippians, including U.S. Senator James Eastland, the powerful chairman of the Judiciary Committee, insisted that the three men were not injured, but were instead part of a hoax designed to bring either federal attention or further ridicule to the state. The *Clarion-Ledger* wrote that "the careful absence of clues makes it seem likely that they are quartered in Cuba or another Communist area awaiting their next task."[77]

Why did the story of the Neshoba murders become so central to narratives of Freedom Summer? At the time, movement people spoke of the men to remind themselves of the real dangers Mississippi harbored. Later, movement veterans remembered the men to recognize the sacrifices that had been made in the name of their goals. The murders are also central to narratives, common in movement memoirs and in many histories of the period, that describe the progress of the civil rights movement toward an attitude of cynicism, if not alienation and despair. A number of the photographs in this volume were taken in Philadelphia and Neshoba County. In the pages that follow, King writes with passion and often with anger of what happened to the men and his sense of the national government's complicity in their killings. At the same time, King realized that the murders represented something like the abyss into which white Mississippi had finally sunk. Following the angry and passionate oratory of CORE leader Dave Dennis, King provided one of the eulogies at James Chaney's funeral on August 7, 1964. His words make it clear that to people involved in Freedom Summer, the significance of the civil rights movement lay not primarily in the attitudes and actions of movement leaders and national policymakers, but instead rather in the collision of entrenched white Mississippi attitudes and the black grassroots movement for social change. King said:

> I come before you now; some of you know me, some of you don't. I'm a Mississippian. I'm the chaplain at Tougaloo College . . . My

parents used to live in Vicksburg before they were run out of Mississippi. By the same kind of people who do this kind of thing and the silent people who, I think, are just as guilty and more damned in their souls because they know it's wrong. I come before you to try to say that my brothers have killed my brothers. My white brothers have killed my black brothers. But here in Mississippi people like Ed King from Vicksburg and James Chaney from Meridian are not supposed to know each other as brothers.[78]

Student volunteers and movement leaders alike worked the rest of the summer in Mississippi with the knowledge that they might not leave the state alive.

The Neshoba County murders caught the attention of the nation in 1964 mainly because Schwerner and Goodman were white; murders of black Mississippians had not occasioned the mobilization of hundreds of U.S. Navy servicemen to comb swamps looking for bodies. Initially, SNCC had strong reservations about using white workers in Mississippi. Some of those concerns were pragmatic. In the Delta, for instance, white workers would be instantly conspicuous, and would draw attention not only to themselves, but also to black movement workers, who otherwise could blend relatively seamlessly with local people; white workers would also draw attention to and threaten danger to those local people who cooperated with the civil rights workers. There were also philosophical reasons for not bringing white volunteers into Mississippi. Some wondered whether northern white workers, with their greater access to education, and perhaps prejudices toward black southerners, would dominate the leadership of local projects. On the other hand, some in SNCC understood that for bet-

ter or for worse, the rest of America would pay closer attention to the fates of white volunteers, some of them the sons and daughters of doctors, attorneys, and congressmen, than they would the rank and file of black Mississippians, whose deaths, let alone beatings and arrests, did not register on the national radar. A sad irony of the murders of the three men, then, is that American racism, manifested here as sudden concern for the missing in Mississippi as soon as some of them were white, brought greater attention to the plight of black Mississippians.

How those murders were remembered by Ed King and others over the next years provide insight into the significance of Freedom Summer. For many white Neshoba Countians, and other white Mississippians, the murders long remained a subject they did not wish to recall. As late as the 1980s, even to mention the killings in a public forum carried a political risk. In 1989 the families of the three slain men organized a memorial service to recognize the twenty-fifth anniversary of the murders. Mississippi Secretary of State and native Philadelphian Dick Molpus was asked to serve as honorary chair of the memorial service committee and to speak at the event. Historian Yasuhiro Katagiri notes that "Molpus was told by some of his closest advisers that his involvement in the commemorative ceremony would be politically unwise." He went anyway. "My heart is full today," said Molpus to the audience. "My heart is full because I know that for a long time, many of us have been searching for a way to ease the burden that this community has carried for 25 years . . . Today we pay tribute to those who died. We acknowledge that dark corner of the past." James Chaney's mother said, "I'm so glad that I lived long enough to see this day come."[79] But not all white Mississippians were ready yet to come to terms, especially if those terms involved a public apology, with the state's violent past. That same year, the state's congressmen (all white, except for Bennie Thompson, a Democrat who represented the largely black Delta district) declined to support a resolution honoring the twenty-fifth anniversary of the deaths of Chaney, Schwerner, and Goodman.

Six years later, Dick Molpus secured the Democratic nomination for governor of Mississippi. Some observers, however, maintained that Molpus's political career in the state was compromised by the apology he had offered in Neshoba County. Kirk Fordice, his Republican rival in the gubernatorial race, obliquely criticized Molpus for his speech at the 1989 Neshoba County memorial service. Before an audience at the politically potent, tradition-rich Neshoba County Fair (just outside Philadelphia), Fordice asserted, "I don't believe we need to run this state for *Mississippi Burning*," a reference to the 1989 film about the Neshoba killings that had riled many white Mississippians with its unsympathetic representation of the state. He continued: "Never apologize! Never look back! Forward together!"[80] Much has changed in recent years, though. The Philadelphia Coalition, a community group of blacks, whites, and Choctaws, was formed in 2004 to foster dialogue and the possibility of racial reconciliation.[81] And Edgar Ray Killen, a sawmill operator, Baptist preacher, and former Ku Klux Klansman, was convicted of three counts of manslaughter for the killings on June 21, 2005, precisely forty-five years after Chaney, Schwerner, and Goodman were murdered. Mississippi newspapers and public officials largely applauded the verdict.

In 2004 Dick Molpus spoke again in Philadelphia of the Neshoba murders. Before an audience that included Philadelphia Coalition members as well as Governor and Mrs. Haley Barbour and U.S. Representative Chip Pickering and his sons, Molpus made it clear that conviction of any one man or small group of men, however necessary for the achievement of justice, would not absolve white Mississippians of responsibility for the past, nor should such verdicts be read as evidence that racial injustice in the state had been consigned to the dustbin of history. Molpus continued.

> [He] complimented the Philadelphia Coalition . . . Then he said he wanted to talk to all the white people in the room, saying "we are all at least somewhat complicit in those deaths" until we face our "corporate responsibility" for the crimes. He pleaded for anyone with information on the murders to come forward to help bring closure . . . "Now is the time to expose those dark secrets" . . . Molpus, with a quiver in his voice, challenged the governor sitting behind him and others like him: "Few politicians today use outright race baiting, but we see the symbols some use and the phrases they utter and everyone knows what the code is—what really is being said." People were on their feet . . . Molpus ended by saying Mississippians must write, or rewrite, our own history: "40 years from now I want our children and grandchildren to look back on us and what we did and say that we had the courage, the wisdom, and the strength to rise up, to take the responsibility to right historic wrongs . . . that we pledged to build a future together—we moved on—yes, we moved on as one people."[82]

The work of Freedom Summer, built upon by a generation of black and white Mississippians, made it possible for a white Mississippi politician to stand before that racially integrated crowd in Philadelphia, Mississippi, to lay out a vision for racial reconciliation and justice, and to call for a continuing dialogue about race and the demands of community.

In the shorter term, though, what did Freedom Summer accomplish? The 1964 elections showed relatively little harvest for COFO's labors. The Mississippi Freedom Democratic Party's challenge to unseat the regular Mississippi Democratic delegation in Atlantic City failed. After much negotiation, and with much acrimony and many accusations and hard feelings to follow, the sixty-four-member MFDP delegation was offered two at-large delegate seats, one of them for Ed King and one for Aaron Henry. That offer prompted Fannie Lou Hamer's famous declaration that "We didn't come all this way for no two seats." President Lyndon Johnson was determined not to alienate other southern delegations, which might have bolted if the Mississippi regulars had not been seated. He instructed Sen. Walter Mondale and United Auto Workers president Walter Reuther to persuade the delegation not to disrupt a convention that Johnson had long anticipated as a further step in making the presidency seem his own rather than an office won by an assassin's bullet. The MFDP delegation ultimately voted not to accept the White House offer. Later Democratic conventions would in fact adopt more democratic and more liberal guidelines for the constitution of delegations, but in August of 1964 many of the MFDP delegates and their allies saw Atlantic City mainly as another chapter in politics as usual.

After 1964, the COFO coalition in Mississippi and similar alliances in other parts of the South and the nation began to fracture. Jeannette King recalls: "We returned to Mississippi [from Atlantic City] exhausted. For me, this was the beginning of the end of the idealist phase of the movement. . . . [In 1965] CORE, SCLC, and the NAACP distanced themselves from SNCC, fearful that SNCC's tactics were too radical to be 'managed.' To me, the Movement in Mississippi was SNCC, but there was no place for a white southerner to fit into the organization as it began to change." Said SNCC's Joyce Ladner, "For many people, Atlantic City was the end of innocence."[83]

Despite their and COFO's attempts, would-be black voters were not registered in large numbers in 1964. However, Freedom Summer and the MFDP did inspire black voter drives in places like Selma, Alabama. The Voting Rights Act of 1965, not the moral suasion or determination of Freedom Summer volunteers and local people, removed the legal barriers to black voting. But of course the violence that the rest of America witnessed in 1964 and 1965 from Mississippi and Alabama, along with Lyndon Johnson's continued ability to draw on the memory of John F. Kennedy, did persuade many in Congress that passage of voting legislation was imperative. And white violence against movement volunteers and local people in Mississippi exacted a fearsome toll. Some of the toll of Freedom Summer is quantifiable. John Dittmer writes that "the summer of 1964 was the most violent since Reconstruction: thirty-five shooting incidents and sixty-five homes and other buildings burned or bombed, including thirty-five churches. One thousand movement people were arrested, and eighty activists suffered beatings. In addition to the Neshoba lynchings, there were at least three other murders."[84] The psychological toll on Mississippians—black and white, pro– and anti–civil rights movement—is harder to measure, but nevertheless was considerable, and would shape politics and culture in the state for years.

In the fall of 1964, approximately 14 percent of eligible black Mississippians voted in the presidential election. To move the percentage of registered black voters from 6 percent of those eligible to 14 percent is not insignificant, given that the registration work was done in an atmosphere of violence that few people outside Mississippi would have imagined. Despite the work of Freedom Summer, however, voting figures that fall showed how far registration work still had to go. In Scott County, for instance, 3,752 African Americans were of voting age, while only 16 were registered; in Walthall County, the figure was 4 out of 2,490; in Chickasaw County, the figure was 1 of 3,054; and in Lamar County, while 1,071 African Americans were of voting age, not one was registered to vote that fall.[85] Still, writes one historian of the MFDP, "The Freedom Party's enduring voter registration drives built a significant black electorate that in 1967 created the first generation of black officeholders and shifted the tenor of white political discourse."[86] Such progress hardly seemed possible in 1963.

Freedom Summer, then, did not bring the end of racial discrimination in voter registration in Mississippi, but it did provide evidence for the national government's need to enforce voting laws. For example, the MFDP provided the House of Representatives with more than six hundred depositions, including more than three thousand pages of documentation, showing that the 1964 campaigns of Fannie Lou Hamer, Annie Devine, and Victoria Gray for Mississippi congressional seats were marked by violence and intimidation. And of course Freedom Summer did not persuade most white Mississippians that their fundamental assumptions about race and community were unsound; racial reconciliation in the state remained and remains a

work in progress. The summer of 1964 did, however, produce lasting results. First, the fact that white college students faced mortal danger in Mississippi was certainly necessary to bring the kind of media coverage that exposed to the rest of America the brutal treatment that black Mississippians had known for generations. That coverage showed other Americans conditions that many would have doubted still existed in the midst of postwar prosperity. Black Mississippians were as much "other Americans" as the urban poor and other "invisible poor" about whom Michael Harrington wrote in 1962. Activist historian Howard Zinn noted the visibility that the project gave to black aspirations in Mississippi: "[F]or the Negroes of Mississippi, in the summer of 1964, as college students from all over America began to join them to help bring democracy to Mississippi and the nation, the long silence was over."[87] Black Mississippians might amend Zinn's remark to say that they had been not so much silent as unheard. Freedom Summer did help to make their voices heard.

Perhaps more important than the national awareness of Mississippi conditions that Freedom Summer brought to American media audiences was the effect that the project had on black Mississippians. It is difficult to overestimate the degree to which basic rights were denied in the state. Over time many black Mississippians accepted or at least acquiesced in their exclusion from the political process. The voter registration efforts that had begun in earnest in the early 1960s eventually bore fruit. By the time of the MFDP's Freedom Vote and Freedom Summer itself, black attitudes had begun to change. A contemporary journalist noted that in covering the state "in the early 1950s . . . the white man was too dangerous and the idea of entering into a relationship with him too foreign for most Negroes. But returning to Mississippi in 1963, it was plain that there had been a change. While there were still many Negroes who acted in the old way, there were also many who did not."[88] By the late 1960s, no white Mississippian could doubt that black Mississippians were determined to vote and to demand other constitutional rights.

Despite the drama of the Atlantic City delegation seating challenge, the real significance of the MFDP's effect on Mississippi politics began to show itself on the local and county levels, despite that party's lack of electoral success in the 1970s. The MFDP chairman, Lawrence Guyot, a Tougaloo graduate, encouraged the participation and indeed the initiative of local people. Then as now, however, the white, conservative Mississippi majority determined how the state fared in presidential as well as most statewide elections. However, black voters accurately assessed the contemporary climate and learned to ask the right questions, sending more and more black elected officials into office. Of Hinds County, one source counseled shortly after Freedom Summer: "The county government is run by a few rich white people. They don't represent poor white people, either, but they *sure* don't represent Negroes!"[89] However, the coalition of the black and white poor that some movement activists hoped to build did not come to pass in Mississippi. And black voters have had two generations now to see that problems such as poverty in the Delta seem to have no solution easily provided by the ballot. But those challenges are not simply Mississippi problems, but rather broader American problems that cannot be laid at the feet of COFO and its allies.

In the years since Freedom Summer, Rev. Ed King has remained a champion of the causes he espoused in 1964. Speaking with King, then, is to be reminded of the deep spirit of Christian reconciliation that animated much of the civil rights movement in the 1950s and early 1960s. If others grew cynical about that goal, King did not. And in recent years, his hopes for interracial cooperation and understanding have certainly become part of the state's cultural and political discourse. King remained active in electoral politics for several years after the summer of 1964. He ran unsuccessfully to represent Mississippi's third congressional district on the Freedom Democratic ticket in 1966 against incumbent John Bell Williams on another interracial ticket; Methodist minister Rev. Clifton Whitley, chaplain of Rust College, ran against Senator James O. Eastland. King served as a member of the now-integrated Mississippi delegations to the Democratic National Convention again in 1968 and 1972, after the MFDP had lost much of its momentum. Historian Chris Danielson writes: "The MFDP struggled after the 1968 Chicago convention to exist as an independent political party . . . The MFDP's leadership either left the state or became preoccupied with other concerns, and the NAACP had more success electing black officials." Politics and movement work was emotionally and physically taxing on King. He recalled: "One reason that I left [Tougaloo]—Jeannette and I left—we were exhausted by '68 when we left the state . . . we left Tougaloo in '67 to do some full time work with the National Council of Churches in the state."[90] The Kings' marriage, as did that of many activists, also suffered from the years of near-constant stress. They divorced in 1986.

In 1972, after a year's study in India at the Gandhi Peace Foundation, the Kings and their two daughters returned to Mississippi, where Ed King continued to speak and work on behalf of causes that he saw as consistent with his longstanding interests in civil rights and racial justice. He became an outspoken critic of abortion, stemming from his conviction that, especially in the South, abortion could be turned to eugenicist ends against African Americans. Given the history of white violence against black bodies that King had witnessed, such a position seems consistent with his previous work. King told a student audience: "Fannie Lou Hamer was the first person to talk to me after *Roe vs. Wade* came down and she said, 'Rev. King, this is another racial thing, this is the answer to the civil rights movement, they are going to get rid of black babies.'"[91] However principled King's stand, it placed him on the opposite side of former allies in the civil rights movement.

In the 1980s and 1990s, King spent a great deal of energy—"fifteen years of my life," he said, opposing the opening of the records of Mississippi's Sovereignty Commission.[92] When the Sovereignty Commission was officially disbanded in 1977 (Governor Bill Waller had vetoed its funding in 1973), its records were to be sealed for fifty years. A number of people, including Ed King and John Salter, filed suit to force an earlier opening of the papers, largely to reveal the details of the state's official opposition to the civil rights movement and its spying on a host of its own citizens. To the surprise of many movement veterans, King subsequently opposed the opening of the papers and signed on with John Salter as a plaintiff in a lawsuit opposing their opening without the protection of personal privacy rights. Believing them to be riddled with lies and malicious gossip, he thought that many of the personal details from the papers deserved to be shielded from the public eye. The papers now have

been opened and digitized and are available on line through the Mississippi Department of Archives and History.[93] While the files are almost certain to have been selectively edited before their opening, they still contained a number of surprises. African American Mississippi memoirist W. Ralph Eubanks was shocked to learn that a friend's father was an informer for the Sovereignty Commission. King said to Eubanks: "What is so ironic, is the Sovereignty Commission is dead; but it is still pushing division among those of us who needed to pass on the legacy of the Civil Rights movement."[94]

As of 2013, King was an associate professor in the School of Health Related Professions at the University of Mississippi School of Medicine in Jackson where he teaches sociology to students who will become medical workers. Along with that teaching, Ed King has spent much of the last few decades reminding people of the significance of the work of Freedom Summer and of the broader civil rights movement. He is an indefatigable speaker, with a special interest in reaching students and others too young to have memories of the 1960s. He has embraced a role as a person charged with keeping memories of the civil rights movement alive to a generation that can scarcely imagine Mississippi as it once was. King has also been extremely generous with historians, whether established scholars, graduate students, or native Mississippians who want to understand the state as it was in the years before they were born. Dozens of books and articles bear witness to this generosity, each listing "Interview with Rev. Ed King" in the footnotes.

He has also been attentive to the memory of his friend Medgar Evers. In 1983 King (and former colleague John Salter) was deeply troubled by a filmed version of Myrlie Evers's memoir, *For Us, The Living*. King particularly objected to the film's heroic representation of the NAACP. Writing to the National Endowment for the Humanities, which provided funding for the film, King said: "The evening of his murder Mr. Evers told me that he was being fired from his job by the national NAACP because he was defying their orders, and by implication, orders from the liberal Democratic White House, to stop the direct action pickets and protest marches in Jackson."[95] King, who throughout the years had retained a sense of irony, appreciated the naming in 2009 of the Jackson, Mississippi, airport for Evers, especially since the airfield itself had long borne the name of Evers's nemesis, Allen Thompson.[96]

The tenth and twentieth anniversaries of Freedom Summer brought no official fanfare in Mississippi, and little coverage by the state's newspapers and television stations. By the 1990s that fact began to change, and as we now reach the fiftieth anniversary of the Freedom Rides, Freedom Summer, and the eventual mass registration of black Mississippi voters, the calendar is becoming filled with reunions, reminiscences, and commemorations by the state and local governments. The events of the 1960s that are being remembered took place within their own context of remembrance, of course. Fifty years ago Americans celebrated the centennial of the Civil War; Mississippi officially celebrated the occasion with pro-Confederate pageantry and oratory that vindicated the cause for which the white South fought. In part due to the civil rights movement, the war they remembered in the 1960s is recalled much differently these days. The official celebration of the Confederacy that prevailed in Mississippi in the 1960s has become much more muted and joined by countervailing stories

of liberation and citizenship. Another measure of changes in the state since the 1960s is the coverage of the civil rights movement in the *Clarion-Ledger*, the state's most broadly circulated newspaper. In the 1960s, the paper, owned along with the *Jackson Daily News* by the segregationist Hederman brothers, provided next to no coverage that was not essentially an antimovement editorial. For example, one headline on the day after the 1963 March on Washington and the speech of Dr. Martin Luther King Jr. (which was not mentioned) was accompanied by a photograph showing only the litter of paper, posters, and other material on the bare steps of the Lincoln Memorial, with the caption "Cleaning Up After the March."[97] Today, the newspaper features the respected investigative journalism of MacArthur Foundation fellow Jerry Mitchell, whose reporting helped to put Byron De La Beckwith, Medgar Evers's accused assassin, in prison.[98]

At the end of 1964, Ed King remarked of the campaign for civil rights in Mississippi: "Some of us may be destroyed emotionally, some of us physically, but there is in this movement the possibility of salvation, the possibility of joy."[99] Viewed especially within the context of his Christian faith, Ed King's work during the summer of 1964 exemplifies the possibility of joy, as well as a willingness to challenge without rancor what seem to be long-odds causes. While Ed King has not received sufficient recognition in many histories of the civil rights movement in the state, movement veterans have increasingly remembered King. The accolades now come regularly from civil rights organizations and churches. In November 2011, King was honored by the National Civil Rights Museum in Memphis, Tennessee, as an "Icon of the Movement," along with Rev. Jim Lawson, Rev. C. T.

Vivian of SCLC, and Ms. Dolores Huerta of the United Farm Workers. "Your involvement and legacy with the leaders of the Mississippi movement and your courageous efforts . . . [deserve] to be told," said his invitation to the event.[100] Earlier, in 2008, *The United Methodist Reporter* remembered King's work. The cross burned at Tougaloo in 1964 was given to Rev. Gerald Forshey and later presented to the Chicago Temple–First United Methodist Church of Chicago in commemoration of the Methodist denomination's struggles with racial integration during those years. King's "outspoken and unwavering support of racial equality led to threats, violence, incarceration and often repudiation for his efforts," noted the newspaper.[101] In 2012 this crucifix was used at Galloway United Methodist Church in a service of racial reconciliation and as an honor to Ed King.[102]

Anne Moody's famous description of Ed King near the end of her searing memoir *Coming of Age in Mississippi* says much about his significance to a generation of black Mississippians and thus about his importance in the state's history. After her graduation from Tougaloo, Moody and her friends were taken out to dinner by King and his wife:

As we were all sitting there eating, I looked at Reverend King. And silently, I asked him to forgive—forgive me for doubting him when he first came to Tougaloo. I think because he was a white native Mississippian almost every student at Tougaloo doubted him at that time. We had never before had a white Southerner on the faculty. His wife, Jeannette, was from Jackson. I remember, I used to look at her going in and out of the chapel after visiting Reverend King there and just hate the thought of a white Southern minister and his wife taking over the most beautiful and cherished build-

ing on campus. Now sitting across the table from them I realized I had more respect for them than any of the white Northern teachers on campus. And for that matter, any white persons I had ever known.[103]

At the end of 1964, Ed King wrote: "The summer program greatly changed Mississippi and the life of both the people who love her, Negro and White, and the lives of those who came to help us."[104] And the summer of 1964 changed Ed King's life as well. King's words in the sentence above serve as a modest but fitting summary of the significance of the stories and photographs in the pages to follow.

NOTES

1. Ed King to Rev. George West, 29 May 1964, T.017: Ed King Papers, Box Nine, Mississippi Department of Archives and History, Jackson, Mississippi [hereafter, MDAH]. "I trust that a number of your students will be involved in the state here before the summer is over," wrote King. West was pastor of Collegiate Methodist Church in Ames, Iowa, home of Iowa State University.

2. For a survey of the civil rights movement in Mississippi, see John Dittmer, *Local People: The Struggle for Civil Rights in Mississippi* (Urbana and Chicago: University of Illinois Press, 1994); for an account that focuses on the Mississippi Delta, see Charles M. Payne, *I've Got the Light of Freedom: The Organizing Tradition and the Mississippi Freedom Struggle* (Berkeley: University of California Press, 1995). For white reaction to the civil rights movement in the state, see Joseph Crespino, *In Search of Another Country: Mississippi and the Conservative Counterrevolution* (Princeton and Oxford: Princeton University Press, 2007). On the summer of 1964, see Doug McAdam, *Freedom Summer* (Oxford and New York: Oxford University Press, 1988), Bruce Watson, *Freedom Summer* (New York: Viking, 2010), and Nicolaus Mills, *Like a Holy Crusade: Mississippi 1964—The Turning Point of the Civil Rights Movement in America* (Chicago: Ivan R. Dee, 1992). In recent years, scholars have produced many studies

of the Mississippi civil rights movement at the city and county levels; see my notes below for citations of those works.

3. *Starkville News*, 1 July 1964; *Clarksdale Press Register*, 3 August 1964. Unless otherwise noted, all newspaper references are to Mississippi newspapers.

4. Nicholas von Hoffman, *Mississippi Notebook* (New York: David White Company, 1964), 21, 23.

5. Elizabeth Martinez, *Letters from Mississippi: Reports from Civil Rights Volunteers and Poetry of the 1964 Freedom Summer* (Brookline, Mass.: Zephyr, 2010), 10.

6. See Charles W. Eagles, *The Price of Defiance: James Meredith and the Integration of Ole Miss* (Chapel Hill: University of North Carolina Press, 2009), 100.

7. For an examination of the increasingly shrill defense of segregation in Mississippi during the late 1950s and early 1960s, see Eagles, *The Price of Defiance*, 80–198. For a contemporary account of those years, see William McCord, *Mississippi: The Long, Hot Summer* (New York: Norton, 1965), 23–49.

8. Payne, *I've Got the Light of Freedom*, 34–35. See Neil R. McMillen, *The Citizens' Council: Organized Resistance to the Second Reconstruction* (Urbana: University of Illinois Press, 1971) and Yasuhiro Katagiri, *The Mississippi State Sovereignty Commission: Civil Rights and States' Rights* (Jackson: University Press of Mississippi, 2001).

9. On the Freedom Rides, see Raymond Arsenault, *Freedom Riders: 1961 and the Struggle for Racial Justice* (Oxford and New York: Oxford University Press, 2006); *Jackson Daily News*, 24 May 1961; Dittmer, *Local People*, 97.

10. King (Ed) Collection, graphic, PI/1984.0018, MDAH.

11. See, for instance, Maurice Berger, *For All the World to See: Visual Culture and the Struggle for Civil Rights* (New Haven: Yale University Press, 2010) and Leigh Raiford, *Imprisoned in a Luminous Glare: Photography and the African American Freedom Struggle* (Chapel Hill: University of North Carolina Press, 2011). Martin A. Berger argues that representations of powerless African Americans actually hindered the cause of reform. See *Seeing Through Race: A Reinterpretation of Civil Rights Photography* (Berkeley: University of California Press, 2011).

12. See Katagiri, *The Mississippi State Sovereignty Commission* and Jenny Irons, *Reconstituting Whiteness: The Mississippi State Sovereignty Commission* (Nashville: Vanderbilt University Press, 2010).

13. Von Hoffman, *Mississippi Notebook*, 51.

14. See Danny Lyon, *Memories of the Southern Civil Rights Movement* (Chapel Hill: University of North Carolina Press, 1992) and Lorraine Hansberry, *The Movement: Documentary of a Struggle for Equality* (New York: Simon and Schuster, 1964). For a review of several recent works, see Allison Berg, "Trauma and Testimony in Black Women's Civil Rights Memoirs: *The Montgomery Bus Boycott and the Women Who Started It, Warriors Don't Cry,* and *From the Mississippi Delta*," *Journal of Women's History* (Fall 2009) 21:3, 84–107; Leslie G. Kelen, ed., *This Light of Ours: Activist Photographers of the Civil Rights Movement* (Jackson: University Press of Mississippi, 2011).

15. Rev. R. Edwin King Jr., interview by John Jones, 8 November 1982, transcript, AU 106, MDAH, 34.

16. Quoted in Charles Marsh, *God's Long Summer: Stories of Faith and Civil Rights* (Princeton: Princeton University Press), 125.

17. See Yasuhiro Katagiri, *Black Freedom, White Resistance, and Red Menace: Civil Rights and Anticommunism in the Jim Crow South* (Baton Rouge: Louisiana State University Press, 2014).

18. Dittmer, *Local People*, 202–203.

19. SNCC, "Mississippi Summer Project," 3; available at www.crmvet.org/docs/dochome.htm#docs mfdp; accessed 20 October 2012.

20. See James Silver, *Mississippi: The Closed Society* (New York: Harcourt, Brace, and World, 1964) and *Running Scared: Silver in Mississippi* (Jackson: University Press of Mississippi, 1984). Among his many other works, see Hodding Carter Jr., *So the Heffners Left McComb* (New York: Doubleday, 1965); P.D. East, *The Magnolia Jungle* (New York: Simon and Schuster, 1960); on Hazel Brannon Smith, see John A. Whalen, *Maverick Among the Magnolias: The Hazel Brannon Smith Story* (Bloomington, Indiana: Xlibris, 2001). See Florence Mars, *Witness in Philadelphia: A Mississippi WASP's Accounts of the 1964 Civil Rights Murders* (Baton Rouge: Louisiana State University Press, 1977).

21. Ed King, interview by John Jones, 20 November 1980, 1.

22. "Two Who Live Dangerously and Like It," *Southern Patriot* 23: 1 (January 1965), 1–3; quotation at 2. The story is a profile of Ed and Jeannette King. *The Southern Patriot* was published by the progressive Southern Conference Educational Fund. Ed King soon became a board member of the SCEF.

23. Edwin King, "Growing Up in Mississippi in a Time of Change," in Dorothy Abbott, ed., *Mississippi Writers: Reflections of Childhood and Youth, Vol. 2:*

Nonfiction (Jackson: University Press of Mississippi, 1985).

24. Ed King, interview by John Jones, 20 November 1980, 2.

25. King, "Growing Up in Mississippi in a Time of Change," 379.

26. Ibid., 380.

27. Marsh, *God's Long Summer*, 120.

28. Jeannette King, "Inside and Outside of Two Worlds," in Faith S. Holsaert and others, eds., *Hands on the Freedom Plow: Personal Accounts by Women in SNCC* (Urbana, Chicago, and Springfield: University of Illinois Press, 2010), 223–230; quote at 223.

29. Marsh, *God's Long Summer*, 120–121. Ed King, e-mail message to author, 24 October 2012. Maddox relocated to Duke University, where he became one of the leading authorities on the sociology of aging and human development. For an obituary, see http://today.duke.edu/2012/08/maddox; accessed 25 October 2012.

30. Marsh, *God's Long Summer*, 121.

31. "Two Who Live Dangerously," 3.

32. Rev. R. Edwin King Jr., interview by John Jones, 8 November 1982, 1, 2, 4.

33. Abbott, ed., *Mississippi Writers*, 715–716.

34. Marsh, *God's Long Summer*, 126.

35. Rev. R. Edwin King Jr., interview by John Jones, 8 November 1982, 4.

36. Katagiri, *The Mississippi State Sovereignty Commission*, 153, 155–156.

37. Dittmer, *Local People*, 235; Ed King, letter to author, 5 November 2012, Katagiri, *The Mississippi State Sovereignty Commission*, 155–157. Brown University notes that the relationship with Tougaloo College had an "uneasy beginning." Brown and Tougaloo continue a formal partnership and exchange program. See http://www.brown.edu/Administration/Brown_Tougaloo/; accessed 22 September 2013.

38. R. Edwin King Jr., "Foreword," in John R. Salter Jr., *Jackson, Mississippi: An American Chronicle of Struggle and Schism* (Malabar, Fla.: Robert E. Kreiger, 1987 [orig. ed. 1979]), viii. See Michael J. O'Brien, *We Shall Not Be Moved: The Jackson Woolworth's Sit-In and the Movement It Inspired* (Jackson: University Press of Mississippi, 2013).

39. Ed King, "Bacchanal at Woolworth's," in Susan Erenrich, *Freedom Is a Constant Struggle: An Anthology of the Mississippi Civil Rights Movement* (Montgomery, Ala.: Black Belt Press, 1999), 27–35.

40. King, "Foreword," viii–ix.

41. Fred Smith to Mrs. Merle Nelson, 12 July 1961; available at http://breachofpeace.com/blog/?p=54;

accessed 12 October 2012. For photographs of the Freedom Riders, see Eric Etheridge, *Breach of Peace: Portraits of the 1961 Mississippi Freedom Riders* (New York: Atlas & Co., 2008). See the documentary *An Ordinary Hero: The True Story of Joan Trumpauer Mulholland*, dir. Loki Mulholland (Taylor Street Films, 2013).

42. *Jackson Daily News*, 24 June 1961; quoted in David M. Oshinsky, *"Worse Than Slavery": Parchman Farm and the Ordeal of Jim Crow Justice* (New York: The Free Press, 1996), 233.

43. Anne Moody, *Coming of Age in Mississippi* (New York: Random House, 1968), 266–267; King, "Foreword," ix.

44. O'Brien, *We Shall Not be Moved*, 284, 286.

45. John R. Salter Jr. to Homer Ellis Finger Jr., 10 May 1963 [first letter]; John R. Salter Jr. to Homer Ellis Finger Jr., 10 May 1963 [second letter]; Reverend R. Edwin King Jr. to Dr. Homer Ellis Finger Jr., 10 May 1963; Civil Rights and Methodism (Jackson), Z1957.000/F, Mississippi Department of Archives and History, Jackson, Mississippi.

46. King, "Growing Up in Mississippi in a Time of Change," 380. See also W.J. Cunningham, *Agony at Galloway: One Church's Struggle with Social Change* (Jackson: University Press of Mississippi, 1980). Cunningham was pastor of Galloway from 1965 to 1966. See also Dalton Carter Lyon, "Lifting the Color Bar from the House of God: The 1963–1964 Church Visit Campaign to Challenge Segregated Sanctuaries in Jackson, Mississippi," Ph.D. diss., University of Mississippi, 2010.

47. Ed King to Mr. and Mrs. Omar Joyce, 29 May 1964, T.017: Ed King Papers, Box Nine, Mississippi Department of Archives and History, Jackson, Mississippi. Anne Moody, *Coming of Age in Mississippi*, in *Reporting Civil Rights, Part One: American Journalism, 1941–1963* (New York: Literary Classics of the United States, 2003), 881.

48. On Gray, see Araminta Stone Johnston, *And One Was a Priest: The Life and Times of Duncan M. Gray Jr.* (Jackson: University Press of Mississippi, 2011); *Hattiesburg American* 28 July 1964.

49. Lyon, "Lifting the Color Bar from the House of God," iv.

50. King, "Growing Up in Mississippi in a Time of Change," 380.

51. Dittmer, *Local People*, 165–167; O'Brien, *We Shall Not Be Moved*, 197–203.

52. King, "Growing Up in Mississippi in a Time of Change," 382, 383.

53. Salter, *Jackson, Mississippi*, 232, 233; King, "Foreword," xii.

54. Michael Paul Sistrom, "Authors of the Liberation: The Mississippi Freedom Democrats and the Redefinition of Politics," Ph.D. diss., University of North Carolina at Chapel Hill, 2002, 31–32. See also Rachel B. Reinhard, "Politics of Change: The Mississippi Freedom Democratic Party and the Emergence of a Black Political Voice in Mississippi," Ph.D. diss., University of California, Berkeley, 2005. See also Anne Cooke Romaine, "The Mississippi Freedom Democratic Party Through August, 1964," M.A. thesis, University of Virginia, 1970. Romaine's thesis contains over three hundred pages of transcriptions of interviews with such figures as Bob Moses, Lawrence Guyot, Allard Lowenstein, Fannie Lou Hamer, Ed King, and Ella Baker. On black voting and political participation in the years before the civil rights movement, see Neil McMillen, *Dark Journey: Black Mississippians in the Age of Jim Crow* (Urbana: University of Illinois Press, 1989), 35–71.

55. On Hamer, see Kay Mills, *This Little Light of Mine: The Life of Fannie Lou Hamer* (Lexington: University Press of Kentucky, 2007); for a transcript of Hamer's testimony before the Credentials Committee at the convention, see http://soundlearning.publicradio.org/subjects/history_civics/say_it_plain/ProfileTranscript_%20Fannie%20Lou%20Ham.pdf; accessed 27 October 2012.

56. Payne, *I've Got the Light of Freedom*, 295. On Aaron Henry, see Aaron Henry with Constance Curry, *Aaron Henry: The Fire Still Burning* (Jackson: University Press of Mississippi, 2000).

57. Aaron Henry–Ed King television speech, 17 October 1963, Sovereignty Commission online, 1-16-1-53-1-1-1; accessed 12 January 2009.

58. Dittmer, *Local People*, 205; *Jackson Free Press*, 30 October 2003, Dennis quoted in Dittmer, *Local People*, 205.

59. Tom Hayden, *Revolution in Mississippi*, in *Reporting Civil Rights, Part One*, 619; "The Mississippi Freedom Democratic Party," n.p., 1964, 8, 325.5 M67B, MDAH.

60. James C. Cobb, *The South and America Since World War II* (Oxford and New York: Oxford University Press, 2011), 93. On Lee and Allen, see Dittmer, *Local People*, 109. For the black registration figures, see "The Mississippi Freedom Democratic Party," 21–22.

61. Hayden, *Revolution in Mississippi*, 619; Payne, *I've Got the Light of Freedom*, 119.

62. On Moses, see Eric R. Burner, *And Gently He Shall Lead Them: Robert Parris Moses and Civil Rights in Mississippi* (New York: New York University Press, 1994).

63. Richard Woodley, "It Will Be a Hot Summer in Mississippi," *The Reporter*, 21 May 1964, 21–23.

64. Martinez, *Letters from Mississippi*, 22. For a memoir by a volunteer, see Sally Belfrage, *Freedom Summer* (New York: Viking, 1965).

65. SNCC, "Information Sheet—Project Mississippi," 2, available at www.crmvet.org/docs/dochome.htm#docsmfdp; accessed 21 October 2012.

66. Hayden, *Revolution in Mississippi*, 624; *Delta Democrat-Times*, 28 July 1964; Jackson *Clarion-Ledger*, 6 July 1964.

67. *Meridian Star*, 12 July 1964.

68. McCord, *Mississippi: The Long Hot Summer*, 64.

69. *Newsweek*, 24 February 1964.

70. McCord, *Mississippi: The Long Hot Summer*, 121.

71. Kelen, *This Light of Ours*, 234.

72. G. McLeod Bryan, *These Few Also Paid a Price: Southern Whites Who Fought for Civil Rights* (Macon, Ga.: Mercer University Press, 2001), 28.

73. Martinez, *Letters from Mississippi*, 12, 7.

74. Ibid., 168.

75. For a near-contemporary account of the Philadelphia murders, see William Bradford Huie, *Three Lives for Mississippi* (New York: WCC Books, 1965). For the 1967 trial of those men accused of the murders, see Howard Ball, *Murder in Mississippi*: United States v. Price *and the Struggle for Civil Rights* (Lawrence: University Press of Kansas, 2004). King quoted in Ball, *Murder in Mississippi*, 3.

76. Woodley, "It Will Be a Hot Summer in Mississippi," 21–22.

77. Rev. R. Edwin King Jr., interview by John Jones, 8 November, 1982, 78, 80, 81; *Clarion-Ledger*, 3 August 1964.

78. Bryan, *These Few Also Paid a Price*, 19.

79. Katagiri, *The Mississippi State Sovereignty Commission*, 232–233.

80. Quoted in Trent Watts, "Mississippi's Giant House Party: Being White at the Neshoba County Fair," *Southern Cultures* 8: 2 (Summer 2002), 38–55; quotation at 50.

81. See the group's website at http://www.neshobajustice.com/; accessed 19 October 2012. See also Micki Dickoff and Tony Pagano, dir., *Neshoba: The Price of Freedom* (Pro Bono, 2010). The documentary also notes the resentment felt by some local whites about the trial "stirring up the past."

82. Donna Ladd, "I Felt the Earth Move," *Jackson Free Press*, 24 June 2004.

83. On the MFDP in Atlantic City, see Dittmer, *Local People*, 272–302; Ladner quoted in Dittmer,

Local People, 302; King, "Inside and Outside of Two Worlds," 229.

84. Dittmer, *Local People*, 251. For a collection of fifty-seven affidavits documenting instances of violence against movement workers and black Mississippians, see *Mississippi Black Paper* (New York: Random House, 1965).

85. Shirley Tucker, *Mississippi from Within* (New York: Arco Publishing Co., 1965), 7. Tucker's figures are drawn from the U.S. Commission on Civil Rights.

86. Sistrom, *"Authors of the Liberation,"* 517. On Mississippi politics in the wake of Freedom Summer, see Chris Danielson, *After Freedom Summer: How Race Realigned Mississippi Politics, 1965–1986* (Gainesville: University Press of Florida, 2011).

87. On the unsuccessful challenge of Hamer, Devine, and Gray for seats in Mississippi's House of Representatives delegations, see Dittmer, *Local People*, 338–341; Howard Zinn, *SNCC: The New Abolitionists* (Boston: Beacon Press, 1964).

88. Von Hoffman, *Mississippi Notebook*, 9, 10.

89. Freedom Information Service, *The Time Has Come to Get That Power: A Political Handbook for the Black People of Hinds County* [1966?], 5, MSSC online 2-163-0-13-1-1-1.

90. Danielson, *After Freedom Summer*, 52; Rev. R. Edwin King Jr., interview by John Jones, 8 November 1982, 31.

91. Ed King at the Bonhoeffer House, University of Virginia, Charlottesville, Virginia, 27 February 2002; transcript available at http://www.livedtheology.org/pdfs/e_king.pdf; accessed 20 October 2012.

92. Rev. R. Edwin King Jr., interview by Trent Watts, 6 March 2009, Jackson, Mississippi.

93. See http://mdah.state.ms.us/arrec/digital_archives/sovcom/; accessed 25 September 2013.

94. W. Ralph Eubanks, *Ever Is a Long Time: A Journey into Mississippi's Dark Past* (New York: Basic Books, 2003), 191. See also Katagiri, *The Mississippi State Sovereignty Commission*, 230ff.

95. Rev. Ed King to Jeffrey D. Wallin, 8 April 1983, Ed King Subject File, MDAH.

96. Rev. Ed King, e-mail message to author, 27 May 2009.

97. *Jackson Daily News*, 29 August 1963.

98. On the *Clarion-Ledger*'s transition from racism to respectability, see *Baltimore Sun*, 5 January 1997. For "Journey to Justice," an archive of Jerry Mitchell's work, see http://blogs.clarionledger.com/jmitchell/; accessed 20 October 2012. On commemoration of the civil rights movement, see Renee C. Romano and Leigh Raiford, eds., *The Civil Rights Movement in American History* (London and Athens: University of Georgia Press, 2006) and Owen J. Dwyer and Derek H. Alderman, *Civil Rights Memorials and the Geography of Memory* (Chicago: The Center for American Places at Columbia College Chicago, 2008). See also Alyssa D. Warrick, "'Mississippi's Greatest Hour': The Mississippi Civil War Centennial and Southern Resistance," *Southern Cultures* 19:3 (Fall 2013), 95–112.

99. "New Generation Making History," *The Southern Patriot* (December 1964) MSSC online 2-158-1-7-1-1-1; accessed 20 October 2012.

100. Beverly C. Robertson to Ed King, 1 April 2011, copy of letter in author's possession.

101. Susan Dal Porto, "Church Civil Rights Leaders Recall Early Struggles," 1; available at http://umc-gbcs.org/faith-in-action/lest-we-forget; accessed 21 October 2012.

102. Ed King, letter to author, 5 November 2012.

103. Moody, *Coming of Age in Mississippi*, 379.

104. Edwin King to Mr. B. J. Stiles, 19 December 1964, T.017: Ed King Papers, Box Eight, Mississippi Department of Archives and History, Jackson, Mississippi.

DOGS

OBSERVATIONS ON MISSISSIPPI IN THE SUMMER OF 1964[1]

REV. EDWIN KING

DOGS ARE AN IMPORTANT PART OF THE MISSISSIPPI WAY OF LIFE. SO IT was in 1964 at the start of Freedom Summer. Dogs are as much a part of the tradition as cotton and kudzu vines, as beauty queens and humble colored folks. Some Mississippi dogs are free and friendly, enjoying the presence of any person. However, many Mississippi dogs act too much like white Mississippi people. Many white dogs (dogs that belong to white persons) hate black people so much that white men joke about it and comment on how their dogs just "naturally can't stand 'Nigruhs,'" not to see them or even smell them. The very presence of a black man will set these white dogs off into tirades of aggressive and hate-filled growling, something that most of these white owners would be too polite ever to express so openly themselves. Over in the black neighborhoods, there are some black dogs who will even bark (more cautiously, but still with some fear and even defiance) at some white salesmen, bill collectors, and sometimes even at policemen. These black dogs are showing something their black owners would never reveal, perhaps not even to themselves.

There are more dogs in white neighborhoods than in black districts. Most people love the dogs. But some blacks are almost paranoid around any dogs in any neighborhoods, as if hinting at the fear they never dare show on the surface (lest they reveal any dissatisfaction with their "place" in life). Perhaps they have long ago smothered any desire to rebel but still feel guilt and somehow know those white dogs might be turned on them for their offense of questioning. Now they dread all dogs, even that old hound sleeping in the cool dust under their black neighbor's porch. They pass their neighbor's home—and dog—with a stick in their hand; in a white neighborhood, where a stick might be unseemly, they cross to the other side of the street rather than pass too near the territory of some white dog or man. Most white men treat all dogs with friendliness and assurance, the confidence of rulers; many blacks treat all dogs with dread and hidden malice, the obsequiousness of servants.

The leaping, pawing, snarling police dog, the German shepherd—Nazi beast, fangbared pet and tool of the white police—had by 1964 come to symbolize white racist power and opposition to the civil rights movement. All America saw the dogs in 1963 in the streets of Birmingham. In the Mississippi movement we had already faced these beasts in Jackson and Greenwood. In Jackson in late spring of 1961, nine Tougaloo College students staged the first demonstration at the whites-only Jackson Public Library. All nine were arrested. Jackson State College students protested these arrests and gathered outside the courthouse for the trial. White police used German shepherd police dogs to drive the students away. There were some persons injured by the dogs, including a prominent black pastor, Rev. Leon Whitney.[2] The story was that the dogs were from the Vicksburg Police Department and had been trained in Missouri by a former German officer. These dogs were named Happy and Rebel.[3] Their handlers enjoyed showing them off to approving white audiences. A few weeks later the dogs were out again to meet the first Freedom Riders, who were quickly arrested at the Trailways Bus Station.[4]

Jackson police used dogs in the fall of 1961 to drive away blacks organized by Medgar Evers to boycott and picket the state fair, which was "White Only" for one week, then open for a day or so for the colored fair.[5] Blue ribbons were given for the finest white chickens and finest black chickens at the "White Only" fair; then blue ribbons were given for the finest white chickens and finest black chickens at the "Colored Only" fair. The same Ferris wheels were used in the closest thing Mississippi ever came to "separate but actually equal." The same fairground in 1963 was turned into a concentration camp–like prison for demonstrators, complete with torture, barbed wire fences, and Nazi-like white guards with rifles and those same dogs on leashes.

We had even used a photograph by Danny Lyon of such beasts on a political campaign poster in the 1963 Freedom Vote, the "mock" election with Aaron Henry for governor and Ed King for lieutenant governor.[6] In this poster a white policeman leads a snarling dog while a black man cowers on the ground. To dare to put a police dog on a SNCC poster was one way to begin to face our fears.

Freedom fighters knew in 1964 we had to stand up to the beasts. So the civil rights movement, which had learned to face so many impossible things with music, even developed a freedom song about dogs. SNCC worker Hollis Watkins brought delight (and secret release?) to all of us in Mississippi by singing a charming and innocent-sounding song about all those dogs who some day would get together to share a bone and sleep in the shade. The song, written by two other SNCC staffers, Bernard Lafayette and James Bevel, helped us overcome this fear and even transform it:

Dog, dog . . . my dog a-love-a your dog
and your dog a-love-a my dog . . .[7]

White Mississippi children grow up surrounded by friendly dogs and cats and take their presence for granted. They have no fear of dogs and need no such songs. By 1964 I shared the terror of police dogs with my movement comrades, but sometimes I recalled my comfortable old world of white Mississippi. We always had dogs and cats around our house in Vicksburg, as did most neighbors and relatives. My favorite childhood pet was Skippy, a very intelligent rat terrier who belonged to my cousin Dottie Lou Shirley and, later, my aunt Marie Tucker. The most exotic pet was the talking parrot of Aunt Alice and Uncle Mack Moore, one that traveled with them when we drove them to Jackson to catch the City of New Orleans or the Panama Limited train for a warmer winter spell in her hometown of New Orleans, where the bird picked up Creole French phrases to add to the English words that so impressed me as a child. The bird traveled the trains in style, a special dark cloak around its cage. They also had a small, almost hairless dog they dressed in sweaters for the worst winter days.

Far out in the Walnut Hills section of Warren County on Bear Creek plantation in Oak Ridge, my aunt Em Henry had a pet goat. I never tired of hearing the stories of the time the goat gave her a butt. When we visited the plantation, we could see deer near the road and often smell skunks. I would peer into the deep darkness of the forests, alert to spot a wolf, or at least a fox. On the plantation there were sheep, horses, mules, cattle, and roaming dogs. Beyond one log cabin smokehouse there was an old carriage house which had survived Sherman and his Yankees, who burned the main home. There was even an ancient unused elegant carriage, but I never got a ride because relatives preferred cars and tractors. I would have preferred they hitch up a team of horses and ride in style with all the friendly dogs racing along beside.

For most children in Vicksburg, horses were a rare and exciting sight, but mules didn't count as adventure since I saw black people riding by almost daily in mule-drawn vegetable wagons. Sometimes kids, black and white, were invited and allowed to ride in the wagons along my home street, but never into the traffic of Washington Street. My aunt Lucy and uncle Johnnie Williamson, the sheriff, lived right across the street from our house at 725 Thomas Street. My cousins there had a squat yellow, almost ugly, chow named Mickey that folks told me was a mean dog. But Benny Ross, my next-door neighbor, my own age and closest friend, liked the old chow and thought it a little fussy, but no more to be feared than any other dog. Even the cows in the pasture behind the houses were reasonably friendly to kids. Down Washington Street at my grandmother Tucker's house, with a backyard that overlooked the river, there were those old photograph albums with pictures of my mother and her sisters in the days before the First World War. My mother could always name the pet dogs in the pictures.

I did not grow up with dogs trained for hunting, since my father did not hunt. (He was not a native Mississippian; he was raised in West Virginia, Ohio, and Louisiana, and those relatives probably were hunters.) Daddy had friends who did hunt, but he said he did not feel right killing deer for sport. He didn't talk about it much and I didn't ask. But most friends and relatives did hunt and I heard the talk of dogs and deer. All my older male cousins certainly were part of the southern hunting tradition and I should have participated in that custom with them and my uncles, but, by the time I was old enough, those cousins were off fighting in Europe or the Pacific.

Close at hand there was some bloodletting, if not quite sport, in the backyard of new neighbors in the summer after my second grade. These were the meanest guys I had ever met—several brothers who were older than I. The older ones picked on the younger ones and were general bullies. They invited me one afternoon to watch while tails were hacked off their puppies. Although I was fascinated, I still felt sorry for the dogs. They recovered. Not so the frogs. The oldest boys, probably high school students, would get the young kids, like me, to help them catch big bullfrogs. I thought that great fun, at first. Then one of the older boys would scoop up a frog from the bucket and, with hammer and nail, attach the live animal to the wooden wall of a back-yard shed. The quivering creature dangled down with one leg stretching from the nail. The boys then lined up to throw knives at the jerking victim. Thud. Thud. Thud. The knives missed and stuck in the wood. Thud. Thud. Thup. Squish, splash. Right on target. Cheers. But sometimes even that did not kill the frog instantly. A nice fat frog was good for several rounds. I was glad they wouldn't let the little kids play that game or even make us scrape up after them. I didn't want to play and that time did not mind the teasing about not being able to handle a knife.

These neighbors never let their dogs inside the house, never even played with them; our cats lived inside and even our dogs came inside in bad weather. These neighbors used their dogs for hunting and breeding, selling off the pups. Sometimes I was allowed to tail along in the woods in the neighborhood ravines on imaginary hunts for panthers or wild turkeys, but the boys only used BB guns and only shot squirrels and robins and sparrows. These kids hated cats and bragged about shooting them. Sometimes the neighbors went off to a real hunt for deer across the river in Louisiana. I was glad not to be

invited. And I was glad when we moved to a new neighborhood.

I preferred my other neighbor, Benny Ross, in whose backyard, sometimes, there were box turtles. School friends, like Lee Davis Thames, had chipmunks in the stacked firewood in the backyard. Barry Henry actually had a horse in his backyard up on Fort Hill overlooking the old river. The only serious hunting my gang went on was for snakes. I would go out with Kenneth Little and his father for target shooting. Mr. Little would warn us to kill only dangerous snakes, like water moccasins and rattlers. I'm afraid most of the snakes my gang killed were harmless chicken snakes or the brightly colored king snakes, which we were convinced were poisonous coral snakes.

In grammar school, some of the boys in these gangs of snake hunts were black; some of these same kids had joined our softball games. By junior high school such contacts were ended. I did notice that all the white boys were quite comfortable around any dogs brought by their white friends, but some of the black kids were very nervous around any dogs. Somehow all the pet dogs seemed to belong to white kids; I can't remember any black kids bringing one of their own dogs. But in those days I never thought much about such things. This was Mississippi. Animals, wild or pets, were part of the scene. Especially dogs.

Most Mississippi dogs are loved just as good companions. However, many dogs have more practical tasks as well. Some dogs are bred for the hunt; some are bred for sport, even the old pioneer amusement of "coon on a log," where the poor dogs try to swim out in some swamp and catch a fiercely fighting raccoon which often bloodies or even drowns some of the dogs before his own death. Meanwhile, the men place their bets, share their liquor, and cheer their favorite animal—sometimes the coon. But this touch of the vile, of the vicious, does not mark the relationship of most people with their dogs, just as it does not mark the relation of most white people with black people.

There are all kinds of dogs; some black people even keep special dogs to smell out water moccasins and bark out a warning. And up in the hills and even in the Delta, there are many "poor whites" who have their hunting dogs and faithful friends like Old Blue, so loved that a man might want to lower his dead dog down into the grave with a silver chain, crying out his name, "Here, Blue. . . ."

But Mississippi never had loving silver chains for black Mississippians—only cold, iron chains. In slavery times and, until recently, on convict chain gangs, the fugitive man who escaped his bonds, desperate for freedom, was tracked down by the sheriff's bloodhounds, their terrible baying summoning the lynch mob, more eager for the death of the nigger in the tree than the coon on the log (whose valor sometimes won the animal's freedom). With the 1961 arrival of the Freedom Riders, white Mississippi began its love of the new-style police dogs, the handsome German shepherds viciously trained in Missouri by a German immigrant in Springfield who was an ex-Nazi guard and dog handler, now advising American police forces.[8]

In the police stations and jails, these dogs were kept on long chains that added an awful rattling, clanging sound to the roaring of the beasts. Imprisoned movement people were forced to pass near the dogs. (The growling of the dogs was never as horrible as the laughter of the police.) Once I thought that the dogs actually would kill me. In the winter of 1964, white police were waiting, as often happened,

outside the gates of Tougaloo College. I was driving and the police instantly followed us all the way into downtown Jackson. Two students, Ida Hannah and Joan Trumpauer, were with me.[9] We had all been in jail before and, reasonably, assumed this time we were on the way to jail. I made a fruitless effort to avoid yet another false traffic charge (which meant jail and heavy fines). Several miles later the familiar flashing police light finally came on. I stopped and was told to follow the police into the underground parking lot of the city jail. This was familiar territory where many friends had been beaten. Far across the unusually empty parking lot floor was the elevator, where even more torture and beatings were routine. The arresting officers ordered the three of us to stand next to my car. The white officers walked to the other side, then a voice cried out, "Let the DOGS kill 'em!"

We heard the ferocious barking and howling of the police dogs. The dreaded German shepherd monsters were charging down on us. We backed against my car; there was no place to run. Two immense dogs leaped towards us, lunging up at our faces and throats. I held my breath and said a silent prayer. The women screamed; the dogs snarled; the police laughed.

The dogs were still on their chains held by the delighted policemen who had not actually released them. The front paws and teeth of the beasts were no more than a few feet away from us. Had one of the women stumbled and fallen towards the dogs, she would have been killed. Had I tried to run or to hold off the dogs, I would have been killed.

More policemen entered the parking garage and their laughter mingled with the growls of the dogs and the clanging of their chains on the concrete floor; all the combined noise reverberated throughout the room. I wanted to scream but did not dare because of the awful feeling that I might never be able to stop.

What a relief it was to be placed in that dreaded elevator where you could almost see the blood stains. This time we were not beaten . . . and no dogs rode up with us. We were taken to the familiar place for mug shots and the standard cursing, then jailed on a false traffic charge. A few hours later, a movement attorney posted our bond and we were released.

The same German shepherd police dogs were used to control black demonstrators and to entertain white audiences. Jackson police officers were often the feature attraction at white civic club luncheons or ladies' teas, presenting their gentle, obedient beasts through their favorite tricks and explaining their efficiency at demonstrations. The white men in the audience snickered and applauded; the white ladies giggled demurely. (Perhaps the old Romans and their wives similarly enjoyed visiting the subterranean zoo at the Coliseum, admiring the lions in their cages, mocking the martyrs in their cages. But did the Romans ever bring a wild bull to tea? Or even a satiated lion to a dull orgy? But, perhaps, the Romans never had a businessmen's civic club luncheon or even a chapter of the Women for Constitutional Government.[10])

These social events featuring the white dogs were duly noted by the *Jackson Daily News*, which on Sept. 7, 1963, had this headline and reporting:

POLICE DOGS PUT THROUGH PACES AT MEET

Deputy Chief of Police A. H. Williams and Officers D. F. Fondren and L. J. Fisher presented a police dog program to the Northwest Jackson Civitan Club at its weekly meeting.

Deputy Chief Williams spoke on the basic and psychological aspects of the additions of police dogs to the Police Department.

He said they are of great value in helping to aid law enforcement.

Officers Fondren and Fisher put their dogs through maneuvers for the group.

The guests were introduced by Dr. Edwin Payne. President Abe Rotwein presided.

(The only things missing from the article were the names of the local clergy who gave the opening prayer, the blessing over the food, and the benediction. When I read the article I did notice, with relief, that nothing was said about a minister blessing the animals or anointing them for their special God-appointed tasks.)

The white public loved the white dogs almost as family members. Obituaries for the dogs very properly listed their names, the causes of death, and surviving (human) family members. On March 11, 1965, the *Jackson Daily News* reported:

TWO POLICE DOGS DEAD

Death has claimed two of the six dogs used in organizing a police canine corps here nearly four years ago.

"Rex," handled by Patrolman John Freeman, died Tuesday of leukemia. Patrolman Cecil Reeves' "Griffin" had become the victim of heart worms a few days earlier.

Both German shepherds were about six years old.

Deputy Chief A. H. Williams said substitute pups had already been purchased from a Missouri kennel [used] when racial demonstrations erupted here four years ago.

Policemen kept the dogs in their homes as family pets when they were not on duty.

The four remaining dogs are still on the job, Williams said.

(And I wondered if the final line had been omitted by error, stating that "in lieu of flowers, donations may be made to your local S.P.C.A. or K.K.K.")

In late 1963 and early 1964, at the intellectual and cultural center of the state, the University of Mississippi, there were no black students. James Meredith had graduated in August 1963. Before Meredith's graduation, the federal troops withdrew from campus; after his graduation, the marshals left as well.[11] The next black student was soon forced out. The few white moderate students at Ole Miss, such as *Daily Mississippian* editor Sidna Brower, were so harassed by the *Rebel Underground* and many of their fellow students that some feared for their very lives.[12] White liberal and moderate faculty members were criticized; white liberal and moderate students were caught and beaten. One night the pet kitten of a known moderate student was killed and left in the dorm room as some kind of warning sign, more sick a sign than a burned cross.

Ivan, a great red Irish setter, came to Mississippi from another college town, Moscow, Idaho. He belonged to Lois Chaffee, a white CORE worker and Tougaloo College professor, whom he often accompanied to the COFO office.[13] They had lived in Mississippi for two years. Once, in the spring of 1964, Ivan needed some minor medical treatment and was taken to a local white veterinarian, who gladly did the needed work and praised the beauty and intelligence of the dog. A few weeks later Lois and Ivan returned to the same vet. This time the vet accused the owner and the dog of being outside agitators and refused the medical treatment. It seems the po-

lice had informed the veterinarian about Ivan and Lois.

Ivan was well known to the police, who kept a constant watch on people and friendly dogs in the movement. On the first day of Freedom Summer, up in Neshoba County, three men were killed. The next morning, in Jackson, two white policemen were cruising in their police car near the COFO Freedom House when they spotted Ivan crossing a street. The police car deliberately chased the poor dog for almost half a block, and then struck him. As disgusted black neighbors watched, the poor dog pulled himself out of the gutter before the police could complete their effort to back their car over him. Ivan managed to drag himself over to the side of his home, the Freedom House, and gave one long, lonely cry; then he crawled into the darkness beneath his master's room to die.

And, on the very last day of Freedom Summer, at the end of August, down in McComb a white family was packing their belongings, preparing to move away from their home and shattered lives. This was Red and Malva Heffner, one of whose daughters had just ended her reign as Miss Mississippi. The Heffners, being good Christians and good Americans, had made an effort to understand the racial turmoil in their community, and to meet some of the white people in the McComb project (who had been bombed the third night after their arrival).[14] They invited a white civil rights worker and a white minister into their home for dinner and conversation. Once the Heffners did begin to understand why the workers were in McComb, they made mild efforts to protest the terrorism and police state conditions of their hometown. Earlier in the summer, they had refused to participate in Help, Inc., the new neighborhood warning system (a business of flashing lights or auto horn signals), and other white preparations for Freedom Summer. As Red Heffner put it, the organizers of the Carroll Oaks subdivision's warning system presumed that civil rights workers in McComb would likely come "into our neighborhood creating a disturbance, destroying our property, or raping our wives."[15] Their neighbors marked the Heffners as suspicious people. Now their attempts at moderation were too much. They were forced to leave town—and the state.[16] Few old friends dared even say farewell. Two families were courageous and showed some sympathy; their pet cats were poisoned. The Heffner family's final task at their old home was to bury their dog, Falstaff, a little dachshund, also poisoned, for this Freedom Summer was a time of poison in white Mississippi.[17]

The Mississippi woods and fields, the swamps and river bottoms, are full of all kinds of animal life, from alligators to deer and bear and fox, even legendary panther and wolf. It is the dog that links the domestic life of Mississippi to the forest life. The dog is honored, as is all animal life. But violence and death are never far away. The dogs of Mississippi are often victims when they get in the way of some human need—like speed. The highways and back roads of the state see a daily slaughter of animal life. Dogs lead the list of victims. It is hard to travel far in Mississippi without seeing the bodies of dogs on the road or in the nearby ditches.

But it is not just dogs. The roads sometimes seem to have carcasses for mileage markers, from the black silhouettes of big frogs to the various mutilated yet still recognizable remains of all the other animals of the land—cats, chickens, skunks, possums, squirrels, raccoons, rabbits, turtles, hawks, snakes, and armadillos in their shattered, use-

less armor. Sometimes the carcasses are deer. Sometimes valuable livestock such as pigs, mules, and cows are the victims. And, sometimes, black men are the victims, their bodies found by the roadside with no witness to say if death came by accident or the random design of white hate. One other vision the traveler in Mississippi cannot avoid, slowly circling in the air or waiting by the roadside, are the buzzards, the southern vultures. It is a fertile land for them. For many generations there has been a smell of death in the Mississippi air. And so it was, in 1964, in Freedom Summer.

NOTES

1. "Most of the 'Dogs' essay was written around 1970." Ed King, e-mail message to Trent Watts, 8 June 2010. All footnotes in this essay are by Trent Watts.

2. Whitney was the pastor of Farish Street Baptist Church in Jackson. See "Landmarks of American Democracy Historical Sites," available at http://www.jsums.edu/hamer.institute/PDFs/Landmarks%20Guide.pdf; accessed 23 November 2011. "A Negro minister, S. Leon Whitney, was bitten by one of the German police dogs." See (Hendersonville, NC) *Times-News*, 24 March 1961.

3. Susan Orlean, *Rin Tin Tin: The Life and the Legend* (New York: Simon & Schuster, 2011), 264. The dogs were trained in Springfield, Missouri. See note 8, below.

4. John Dittmer, *Local People: The Struggle for Civil Rights in Mississippi* (Urbana and Chicago: University of Illinois Press, 1994), 90–99.

5. Ibid., 117.

6. Danny Lyon was a staff photographer for SNCC. For samples of his work, which include some of the most iconic SNCC images, see Lorraine Hansberry, *The Movement: Documentary of a Struggle for Equality* (New York: Simon & Schuster, 1964). On the Freedom Vote, see Dittmer, *Local People*, 200–207.

7. The lyrics appear to be based upon the song "My Dog Loves Your Dog" from *George White's Scandals* (1934), dir. Thornton Freeland and

Harry Lachman. See http://www.imdb.com/title/tt0025166/; accessed 23 November 2011. "My dog loves your dog / And your dog loves my dog / If our doggies love each other / Why can't we?" See http://alles-uke.de/BluePages/mydogloves.htm; accessed 23 November 2011.

8. "'Happy' and 'Rebel,' charter members of the Vicksburg Police Department's canine corps, are making the Jackson Police Department's orders to racial demonstrators more meaningful ... Since their arrival here Tuesday, the animals have spearheaded the disbursement of two major Negro demonstrations . . . Harry Nawroth of Springfield [Missouri], the former Nazi storm trooper who trained killer Dobermans to guard Hitler's airports, trained both 'Happy' and 'Rebel.'" (Jackson, Miss.) *State Times*, 30 March 1961. The photograph accompanying the story shows one of the dogs ripping the sleeve of "an unidentified Negro" wearing a coat and tie. The demonstrators are described as "noisy bystanders." The photograph is captioned "Dog Routs Negroes." See also "Along the N.A.A.C.P. Battlefront," *The Crisis* (May 1961), 291–293. "When NAACP field secretary Roy Wilkins protested to Mississippi Governor Ross Barnett on the [use of police dogs on demonstrators], Barnett told a Jackson newspaper, 'I don't know a thing about the facts. I have so many things that are . . . *more important* to attend to'" (293).

9. Ida Hannah was one of three Tougaloo College students arrested in October of 1963 for attempting to attend services at Jackson's Capitol Street Methodist Church. "[Ed King's] strategy in the months leading up to the summer of 1964 was to crack the church's closed doors in hopes that a breakthrough would shake the foundations of the state's public institutions, social practices, and political establishment." See Charles Marsh, *God's Long Summer: Stories of Faith and Civil Rights* (Princeton: Princeton University Press, 1997), 130, 134–137. Joan Trumpauer, a white Tougaloo College student from Virginia, had been a Freedom Rider, was arrested for that activity in Jackson in 1961, and was active in various other Jackson-area desegregation efforts. See Dittmer, *Local People*, 116, 162. On Trumpauer, see Loki Mulholland, dir., *An Ordinary Hero: The True Story of Joan Trumpauer Mulholland* (Taylor Street Films, 2013).

10. "The [Women for Constitutional Government] sprung from a meeting of three influential white women in Greenwood, Mississippi, the Monday morning following the [1962] violence in Oxford. The women were horrified that state business leaders called for peaceful compliance with no statement supporting Governor Barnett ... Florence Sillers Ogden—a syndicated newspaper columnist, the sister of the longtime Mississippi Speaker of the House Walter Sillers, and one of the three women at the initial meeting in Greenwood—emphasized that conservative issues went beyond the defense of segregation. 'Our constitutional rights have been swept away by armed might,' she warned." Joseph Crespino, *In Search of Another Country: Mississippi and the Conservative Counterrevolution* (Princeton and Oxford: Princeton University Press, 2007), 77.

11. See Charles W. Eagles, *The Price of Defiance: James Meredith and the Integration of Ole Miss* (Chapel Hill: University of North Carolina Press, 2009), 421–424, 435. See also David G. Sansing, *The University of Mississippi: A Sesquicentennial History* (Jackson: University Press of Mississippi, 1999), 309. African American student Cleve McDowell was arrested on September 23, 1963, for carrying a handgun on campus; he was subsequently expelled. In June of 1964, Cleveland Donald transferred to Ole Miss from Tougaloo College under court order.

12. The *Rebel Underground* was "an anonymous alternative paper that began appearing on campus in February 1962." See Eagles, *The Price of Defiance*, 115, 405–406.

13. Chafee was one of the demonstrators who integrated the lunch counter at the Woolworth's drugstore on Capitol Street in Jackson on May 28, 1963. See Dittmer, *Local People*, 162.

14. On the Freedom House bombing, see Dittmer, *Local People*, 267.

15. Nicholas Von Hoffman, *Mississippi Notebook* (New York: David White Co., 1964), 64–78, quotation at 68. "Some Help, Inc., members may have seen Red Heffner's absence from the organization as a belittlement of their concerns, or his attempts to mediate the town's troubles as the officious efforts of a parvenu." Crespino, *In Search of Another Country*, 122.

16. "Within two months Red's insurance business was a shambles, his wife and children were ostracized, and the family's pet dog was poisoned. Finally, on September 5 [1964], they moved away from McComb." Dittmer, *Local People*, 305.

17. See Hodding Carter, *So the Heffners Left McComb* (Garden City, N.Y.: Doubleday, 1965). See also Mac Gordon, *Hometown: A Remembrance* (Magnolia, Miss.: Magnolia Gazette Publishing Co., 2011), 146–148, 164–166, 198–204.

PHOTOGRAPHS

1. Pratt Memorial Methodist Church—Press Conference. M. L. King speaks for MFDP [Mississippi Freedom Democratic Party], Jackson, Miss., July, 1964

This is Pratt Memorial Methodist Church,* now part of the Mississippi United Methodist Church, which is racially integrated; at the time, of course, the Methodist churches were not. The pastor of this church was Rev. Allen Johnson. We in the movement had invited Martin to help us promote the Mississippi Freedom Democratic Party, which we had established earlier that year; that was our way of focusing on voter registration. We had been trying voter registration heavily for the preceding three years and failed to register very many people. There had always been interest in voter registration in the black community and so in certain places throughout Mississippi like Vicksburg, Greenville, Clarksdale, and perhaps on the Gulf Coast, some educated middle-class blacks had always been able to vote. These were usually people who owned property—never in large enough numbers to upset anything—but they were always there; that's important to note. And even in the hardest areas of the state, there had always been black people who were determined that they would vote. There also would have been some voter registration done over the years just by community organizations, especially after World War II. The civil rights movement at this time and place focused on voter registration and citizenship education—that meant teaching people about the political system. One of the earliest famous remarks of Mrs. Hamer—Fannie Lou Hamer—was that when the SNCC workers asked her to try to register to vote, she thought voting was white people's business and had nothing to do with her life. The education program and registration work that began in Mississippi in 1961 was organized by SNCC [Student Nonviolent Coordinating Committee]. However, it had been tough work and by 1964 had not yielded great results.

After the Freedom Rides, the civil rights movement was encouraged by many people, including politicians and friends in the philanthropic foundation world, to go into "noncontroversial" areas like voting as opposed to sit-ins at lunch counters, movie theatres, or the Freedom Rides on the buses. The SNCC people them-

---

* Pratt Memorial United Methodist Church is located at 1057 W. Pascagoula Street in Jackson. The office of the Council of Federated Organizations (COFO) was located two blocks away at 1017 John R. Lynch Street.

selves were divided. A group out of Nashville particularly wanted to continue direct action. Others said we needed to branch out and that we needed to begin reaching people in small towns, not just the black university or college towns. The idea of branching out was supported by SCLC [Southern Christian Leadership Conference]. It was also supported by CORE [Congress of Racial Equality], which was beginning to work with SCLC and SNCC, those two being southern-based organizations. The NAACP thought branching out into voter registration was good. Within SNCC there were some people who realized that things were going to be confrontational no matter which way they went. The government in Washington promised support and help if the civil rights groups would move into voting and away from nonviolent direct action like sit-ins, which they regarded as too confrontational.

While King is always a preacher, he wasn't preaching here. He is praising the workers. He talked about the missing workers in Philadelphia and how much he admires them. He talked about how important it is that we have black and white volunteers. He told them how much it meant that they gave up their summers to help us and that it is significant that they came from colleges everywhere. His tone and his message both asked for our help rather than saying he had come to help us.

—Rev. Edwin King, interview by Trent Watts, June 2, 2009, transcript, December 2009, transcript in author's possession.

2. Pratt Memorial Church, M. L. King speaks for MFDP, Jackson, Miss., July, 1964

The Southern Christian Leadership Conference, led by Martin Luther King, Jr., was very much a part of the voter registration work that summer. They agreed by this time that there should be a stronger concentration on voting and on preparing people to vote. Local people had always been interested in voting, but organizing that vote continued to be difficult. In Mississippi, Medgar Evers of the NAACP had begun working with SCLC, CORE, and SNCC to set up a cooperative way that they could have various organizations doing work and not competing. The background of this work, on which Evers, Bob Moses, and others had been working for several years, is well known and documented in all histories of the movement. People like Amzie Moore, a business owner and activist in Cleveland in the Delta, were pioneers here; Moore had been working for civil rights in the state for many years. In 1961, SNCC decided to start voter registration work in McComb; it's important to note that people in that town like C. C. Bryant were instrumental in that decision. Money was raised through the various civil rights organizations and some local people would provide housing and sometimes feed some of the civil rights workers. The chief money for this campaign came through VEP, the Voter Education Project, coordinated through the Southern Regional Council from major foundation grants. But the early work in McComb in 1961 met with violent resistance, which a number of people in the movement had anticipated.

The MFDP, which of course grew out of the previous year's voting efforts, had been created in 1964 by the Council of Federated Organizations, which included SNCC, SCLC, CORE, and other interested groups. Martin and the SCLC don't get enough credit for their efforts on this initiative, but they were most certainly part of this work. After the Freedom Rides, SCLC left a few staff members, like Annelle Ponder, here in Mississippi and their role was citizenship education. You saw this kind of work in different places in the South. On the Sea Islands of South Carolina and in Georgia at a Quaker training site and other places, specific training in citizenship was done; all of these efforts fed into what we were doing that summer. Our emphasis on voting, justice, and local participation was modeled on what had gone on in the Tennessee mountains at the Highlander Folk School. From the beginning, Dr. King was regarded as part of what we were doing here in the state. Very few Mississippi people, black or white, sufficiently appreciate that. He was not sending in a large number of staff people to work on voter registration and we were not supposed to have demonstrations like Selma. Mississippi was volatile and dangerous; we gave a great deal of thought to how best to proceed here. But from the beginning we regarded King as part of our work and he regarded what we were doing cooperatively as extensions of what his organization was involved in.

He needs credit for SCLC's work in Mississippi that summer. He and his organization knew what we were doing, supported what SNCC and the other organizations were doing, and supported what Medgar and others were doing in the state during that period. Certainly we brought him in primarily to dramatize to local people that this was a major effort. We certainly knew his was the name that would excite people when we had him speak. He was the person who would bring out crowds. The secondary point would have been the national publicity that came from using him. And we did get that when he made this trip.

This photograph would have been taken mid-morning and he is speaking to COFO workers, mostly SNCC, CORE, and Freedom Summer volunteers. The COFO office was a block or so away from the church and there would have been some people there from the neighborhood who heard that Dr. King was at the COFO office and because we didn't have a place for a large group of people there and a press conference there we decided to move over to the church for that.

—*Rev. Edwin King, interview by Trent Watts, June 29, 2009, transcript, December 2009, transcript in author's possession.*

3. Pratt Memorial Church (SCLC-MLK talk), Bob Moses, Euvester Simpson, Jackson, Miss., July, 1964

H ere are Bob Moses and Euvester Simpson; Euvester, a Mississippian, was a member of the SNCC staff, a field secretary. She had also been with Mrs. Hamer and Annelle Ponder in the beating in the Winona jail in June of 1963, which Mrs. Hamer spoke about at the Atlantic City convention later that summer; they had been returning from citizenship training in South Carolina, and were arrested, ostensibly for some breach of segregation policy. Euvester would have been working in the COFO office for the FDP at that point. I had met Bob Moses in the spring of 1963. I had come to Tougaloo as chaplain in January of that year and met him that spring when he was working in Greenwood, but he was also back and forth to the campus at Tougaloo as students were going back and forth to help with SNCC work in Greenwood. Now I had heard of him since he came to McComb in 1961. And I came in and out of the state several times a year and would go to the Tougaloo campus or Medgar's office and was certainly hearing about Moses and his work. Bob was by this point one of the main leaders of COFO and of our efforts in the state that summer.

Major fractures would eventually develop within the movement, and indeed were developing at this point, but not yet with the people you see here in these photographs taken in Jackson. Charles Evers does not take part in Freedom Summer, under instructions from Roy Wilkins and the national NAACP. But at least on a public level, they did not say that those divisions were there. Wilkins comes back to help and also to fight us at the Atlantic City Democratic convention later that summer. Within SCLC, CORE, the National Council of Churches and SNCC, the divisions aren't there, certainly not compared to what would come later. Such divisions did come after the end of Freedom Summer and after the Atlantic City convention. Over the next years, of course, SNCC begins to have serious internal debates over leadership and strategy, particularly about nonviolence and the place of white staff in the organization. But at this point very few people understood—local people don't—that Roy Wilkins and the national NAACP would not support Freedom Summer. It's important to remember that not everyone who would later be remembered as a civil rights activist was on board with what we were trying to do that summer.

This photograph and many of these others were taken in mid-to-late July; the Freedom Summer project officially began on June 21, the same day that the men in Philadelphia, Chaney, Goodman, and Schwerner, turned up missing. At this point the men are still considered missing. I think all of us in the movement assumed that they were dead. Certainly everyone knew that the stakes were that high. In retrospect we said "only" those three workers were killed out of the staff. The actual tension at that time, of course, was that it still could happen to anyone. The bodies had not been found. But the work has begun; the Freedom Schools are going. We've got beautiful reports from all over the state. We have small places asking if they can be part of it. We had experienced that groundswell of support with the Freedom Vote in the fall of 1963.* We thought we would work in about a dozen places, but as those efforts progressed over a few weeks period, we had over

---

* For a campaign poster showing Aaron Henry as candidate for governor and Ed King as candidate for lieutenant governor, see http://mdah.state.ms.us/arrec/digital_archives/sovcom/result.php?image=/data/sov_commission/images/png/cd01/001095.png&otherstuff=1|16|1|71|1|1|1|1076|; accessed 1 May 2011.

one hundred towns around the state say we want to be in this. So again the local people were very ready to do things. They were ready to follow our instructions on what a political party was and they were excited that they would have a voice in it. But we still wanted each county group doing the same things for technical reasons and consistency in training them.

—*Rev. Edwin King, interview by Trent Watts, June 2, 2009, transcript, December 2009, transcript in author's possession.*

4. Jackson, Miss., 1964—July, COFO office, M. L. King talks to staff

This photograph would have been taken in the COFO office on Lynch Street in Jackson. The map of Mississippi on the wall behind Dr. King shows the five congressional districts into which the state was then divided. We had the work in the state that summer organized between the civil rights groups that way. The fourth congressional district was for CORE; that district took in a number of eastern counties, including the Meridian area, where Mickey and Rita Schwerner went to work. SNCC would have had responsibility for four districts and CORE one. SCLC was cooperating everywhere and we welcomed any help we could get from the NAACP anywhere; that cooperation was a matter of principle, but was also practical, because of the need for manpower throughout the state. Chaney, Schwerner, and Goodman, the three volunteers who disappeared in Neshoba County, were technically not with SNCC, but rather with CORE. In the Jackson office we would have had a few paid SNCC people, but most of them would have been summer volunteers. Dr. King's visit here was again to identify with the workers, to lend support, and to get a firsthand view of the work that we were doing. He certainly didn't have to persuade any of these people that what we were doing was important. His visit was to show his symbolic identification with them. In the office that day people did things like point out on the map places like Greenwood, for instance, and highlight what activities were going on in different places. Neshoba County is indicated by the small dark circle on the map just above the head of Dr. King.

—*Rev. Edwin King, interview by Trent Watts, June 2, 2009, transcript, December 2009, transcript in author's possession.*

Despite our belief in non-violence—and that belief and practice should not be sold short—there was a lot of self-defense [and] protection in the black community, there always had been . . . now, those who were purest on non-violence would not carry weapons, but others would defend their homes and churches, especially the black people who had volunteers. Those local people who had black and white workers living in their homes would stand guard over their churches and over their homes at night. So I think that the Klan types and the federal government knew that blacks were going to fight back, if their homes were attacked, and that the possibility of violence and bloodshed were always there. I know that in 1964 there was a lot of debate about a McComb project and whether we should reopen that, given the extreme violence that work there had met in 1961. The decision about McComb was in the context that if we don't go back there, then there probably would be more violence there than if we do, and that whites there and throughout the state would believe that with enough violence, the organizing work would go away. What we would have to do, then, was go in and face it.

With the McComb thing, I was the one pushing hard that we open organizing efforts there. Bob Moses, who knew the area well, was very concerned that people would die. Bob wanted to go and stay there, yet he worried that he could not risk his life, as the overall leader of the project. We expected that people at the level of leadership of Bob and lieutenants like Stokely Carmichael, Lawrence Guyot, and others like that that they would probably be singled out and assassinated. You couldn't let those people go into a situation that was almost certain death and the way we resolved things like McComb was that people would go at some point in the first few days or first few weeks. It may have been a kind of roulette, but you would go to be with the people. We hoped everyone would understand that the people accepting responsibility to be in places like McComb full time had a job to do there and there were others who had a job to do in the Jackson office, or some other place. We were not abandoning them, we were not sending them out to do something we wouldn't do, but it was something that we shouldn't do at that moment.

—*Rev. R. Edwin King, Jr., interview by John Jones, November 8, 1980, transcript, July, 1982, 85, 87–88, Mississippi Department of Archives and History, Jackson, Mississippi.*

5. COFO office staff listening to talk by M. L. King, Jessie Morris, Mary King—SNCC and COFO, Jackson, Miss., July '64

This photograph is again the COFO office on Lynch Street. It would be interesting to see what is on the bulletin board behind these people; these papers may just be bureaucratic and say third district, fourth district something, but it would be interesting to see what actually is on those notices. We kept that office open twenty-four hours a day. So we had a WATS line and in any emergency anywhere in the state people could call in to the central office. And to my understanding the only reason that the office did not get bombed is because we had people in it all the time. We did have incidents where people were beaten standing in front of it, and we were always aware that we were a conspicuous target. However, I met one of the Klansmen who had been keeping an eye on our work—just as a Christian minister I went out of my way to begin talking to him on the phone when I would get hate calls. Eventually I met him and stayed in touch with him over several years. And probably six to eight years after that summer I mentioned to him that it always seemed strange to me that the office wasn't ever bombed. And he said, "Well, Reverend King, I just had my principles and I just don't believe in bombing something with somebody in it and we came by there many times, and I told the other guy—look, you can see those people in there." You couldn't really see the people in the office because we had the window blocked a little. I believe his story, but I also know very well that there were others who would bomb a place with people inside even if he wouldn't.

This wasn't at night, however; this was mid-morning. The building just didn't have many windows and the front window had been partially closed in or something just for security, which is why it seems so dark in there. Now the first time that you and I looked at this photograph you remarked that having a black man and white woman working together like this is precisely what white Mississippi dreaded. I'd never thought of that. Mary King here, who worked in communications for SNCC that summer, is southern, of course. Her father is a Methodist minister who I think had had to move to the Midwest because of his progressive ideas. But her roots were southern. She lives in Virginia now, I believe. In the first year we would not let white women work on projects with black men in places like the Delta. First, we tried to say we wouldn't even let white men like Bob Zellner work there, but very quickly they were needed. Jane Stembridge, a white southerner and long-time member of SNCC, worked in Greenwood—there was some hesitancy from a number of quarters, but the women were willing and they were needed. It's just interesting to me that I never thought of those two people as black and white. We had already transcended considerations like that within SNCC, so it seemed, and despite my relatively young age, I was an elder. I did consider myself SNCC; formal organizational affiliations seemed to matter less that summer than they would later. Then, we were trying to build a beloved community. And I would hear many philosophical and religious and theological talks as well as strategy sessions. We wanted to live a life of loving each other that one day we thought America could find. But at the time I certainly was not taking the picture because I was conscious of this being a black man and a white woman working together.

—*Rev. Edwin King, interview by Trent Watts, June 2, 2009, transcript, December 2009, transcript in author's possession.*

6. Jackson, Miss., July, '64, COFO office, Bob Weil

That's the office WATS line. We had cheap long distance rates because we paid an overall rate for it. We had lists with every office in the state—even codes, to try to preserve some semblance of secure communication—that's probably what some of these things are hanging on the wall. So people throughout the state would call in, then we would call back and the long distance bill would be on us. And we had code names for every office because we assumed, as we always had to, that the line was not secure. That's Bob Weil; he was in our Mississippi public relations office.

In the office that day, Dr. King was there, but the normal daily work was going on. One of the reasons that I took some of these photographs is that I had a real feeling that this was a historical scene. On the one hand, it looks very normal and it looks like a college-age people's office, but it was very well structured, managed, and doing very dramatic work. A few months earlier working out of that office on public relations was somebody from the *Yale Daily News* named Joe Lieberman, probably at that same desk. During the Freedom Vote in the fall of 1963, journalism was a skill Lieberman had and so we had him working on public relations.

We also had an American map on the wall so that we had information in case of disasters or in case of just routine arrests. Part of the information every volunteer had to give us was their college hometown and the college newspaper and their hometown and their hometown newspaper. So cynically, we might say well, look, we haven't had a disaster from Montana. It's about time somebody from Montana was arrested. Now what was that paper in Great Falls? We could laugh a little while at the same time you'd be worried that they were going to be beaten in jail. Or we might say oh heck, we've had twelve California people arrested; we don't have any from Arizona.

A northern white student being arrested was news in Ohio or in Colorado, whereas another black Mississippian being arrested was not. We understood that we had to get the support of Middle America. It took us several years to build it. But it had to be built on something more substantial than Selma marches and that kind of thing. Those were needed, but there was weekly stuff—less dramatic, perhaps, but just as important in its way—like sending speakers out. We sent people out all over the country. I would go out with Mississippi black people or I'd go out alone sometimes just to a church.

In a few places around the country we had Friends of SNCC offices. And these were usually people who had helped in the summer of 1961 around the Freedom Rides or 1962 or 1963. We had Friends of SNCC in the San Francisco Bay area, in the Detroit area, in Chicago, in Boston, probably in New York, so those were the groups we started with as we looked for volunteers to staff our work that summer. Schools like Yale and Stanford were heavily represented in the group of summer volunteers because they had helped with the Freedom Vote in the fall of 1963. Contacts we had made in this earlier work, mainly through college chaplains, were one of the major forms of entrance into the Freedom Summer volunteer efforts.

—*Rev. Edwin King, interview by Trent Watts, June 2, 2009, transcript, December 2009, transcript in author's possession.*

7. Jackson, Miss., July, 1964, COFO office—staff listening to talk by M. L. King—Emmie [Schrader]

Now Mary King worked on public relations out of the Atlanta SNCC office with Julian Bond, but they came in and out of Mississippi and probably would have come because Martin was making this trip. And one of her tasks would be getting in touch with national media people and telling them when something was really important enough for them to be there in the state.

I had an odd incident a few weeks ago. It involved one of the private academies here which were started as all-white schools of white flight. Some of them claimed they had little token starts as private grammar schools fifty years before, of course. This school honored the Freedom Riders. They hosted Joan Trumpauer. She was in the Woolworth sit-in in May of 1963, and is pictured in the recent book on the Freedom Riders. The school band played a piece of music composed by the band director Bruce Carter's son Corey, a student at the University of Southern Mississippi. The song was about courage and was dedicated to Joan. So she was down here a month or so ago for that.* A white friend of mine was also there. He is ten years younger than Joan and is a very liberal lawyer here in Jack-

---

* See *Clarion-Ledger*, 3 April 2009. The school was Jackson Academy. For photographs of Trumpauer and the other Freedom Riders, see Eric Etheridge, *Breach of Peace: Portraits of the 1961 Mississippi Freedom Riders* (New York: Atlas & Co., 2008).

son—he's been very active with the ACLU and other causes like that. He knew the band director at the school. We were talking about things that have changed and I recalled how back in those days somebody like Joan had to be very careful if she was driving into the Delta or even off the Tougaloo College campus. I said I can remember times when I would be put on the floor of the backseat since I was the only white person in the car or on some occasion when I might have a clerical collar on and have been very visible and we needed to get where we were going to speak without incident to tell people not to be afraid. You didn't want to disappear along the way because that would ruin your message. But I told the lawyer about crouching on the floor and also that there were other times when you might have a white man or a white woman in the car and also a black woman and going through most towns the black woman would need to put a handkerchief on her head. And my friend, a Harvard-educated native Mississippian, some ten years younger than Joan, was just appalled and said, well, that is so condescending, I don't believe that ever happened. Well, it did happen. I know SNCC women who would put a bandanna on their head and start shuffling and telling the police, "Lawd, Lawd, Mr. Policeman, I don't want any of them civil rights workers in my house." Well, Gandhi would have said always be honest, but I imagine there were some people who would shuffle in the Indian freedom movement, too. But I realized what a change we have seen since those years. This guy matured in the 70s—he would have been junior high or high school in the 60s—already the world had changed so much for him that he thought it was just condescending and insulting to make a black woman put on a bandanna instead of standing up to the police and getting killed. One hears stories too of black men with good cars keeping a chauffeur's cap handy. It is condescending if you had to do it, but it is wonderful that the world could have changed so much that somebody can't imagine it.

—Rev. Edwin King, interview by Trent Watts, June 2, 2009, transcript, December 2009, transcript in author's possession.

8. Jackson, Miss., July, '64, COFO staff listening to M. L. King, Jessie Morris, Mary King

The students who came down to Mississippi in 1964 certainly knew they were doing something romantic, dramatic, and different, but that certainly wasn't their only motivation. They also had had to face the fact that they might be jailed or could be beaten because that sort of thing had happened with the Freedom Riders in 1961. By 1964 they knew of course that Medgar Evers had been killed in Mississippi. Several other people were murdered through the winter while we were building up to Freedom Summer. They had all heard about the Birmingham church bombing, where even children were targets. We were actually screening the volunteers and refused a few people who we did not think were prepared for the conditions in the state. The volunteers had to come through contacts we had. Those contacts might be and often were college chaplains, but the Friends of SNCC offices interviewed people at Harvard, Yale, the University of Chicago, and so on. Most people were accepted, but we were trying to spot people who emotionally might not be ready, who weren't facing how serious it was, or who seemed to want to prove too much. So we probably rejected a few good men and a few good women. But again we were aware of the dangers involved and wanted to be sure they were, too.

One of my concerns that others agreed with was that we had to get beyond the

Ivies and Berkeley and Stanford if we were really to reach as broad a spectrum of Americans as we wanted to reach. I was naive in those days. Today, I would say if you can reach the people from the top twelve schools in the country, then the rest of the country doesn't matter so much. But back then I said we're not recruiting everywhere and that's a problem. For instance, I spoke at the University of Wisconsin on behalf of and organized by Friends of SNCC—probably the group out of Chicago. I spoke at the University of Michigan in Ann Arbor and I realized that we were not getting very far beyond Yale when we picked up schools like Michigan and Wisconsin. What about the others? And so I started a push that we use college chaplains and we try to get people from the rest of America. And so that was consciously done. They still would have been disproportionately from New York City, California, and Boston, but we were deliberately reaching out. I started pushing this one school that I recruited where I wasn't sure we ever got a volunteer. It was a Disciples of Christ–affiliated college in central Illinois named Eureka whose most prominent graduate was Ronald Reagan. Again, we were working through college chaplains and trying to reach out to those kinds of places. Still, our emphasis and intention was that we were not going to use these people as volunteers in Mississippi unless they really know what the risk is. If they'd watched television, if they'd read the newspaper—which presumably all of them did—certainly they would have been aware of the coverage that the state was receiving. It would be hard for a bright college student to have no idea of the situation in the state. This is still the spring. We were still recruiting during the late spring of 1964. Recall that November of 1963 was the death of President Kennedy. This was a pretty serious group of young Americans at that time. Nobody consciously talked about the assassination and the general sense of the possibility of violence, but that had to be part of anybody's thinking during that period: what's happening to America?

—*Rev. Edwin King, interview by Trent Watts, June 2, 2009, transcript, December 2009, transcript in author's possession.*

9. Jackson, Miss., July '64, COFO/SCLC visit office, C. T. Vivian

This photograph is still in the Jackson COFO office. Notice on the wall there it reads "The Opposition" and just under it there is a Klan poster of some kind. I am hoping that at some point people will give me some posters like that that they tucked away in their attic. I have four grandchildren—I'd like to give them posters from the Freedom Vote in 1963. I remember one Klan poster particularly; it was a wanted poster and Anne Moody's name is on it, my name is on it, Medgar Evers's name is on it and by that point his name was crossed out. I used to have a copy, but I don't have one anymore. Having the poster on the wall there would have been our way of laughing at handling the danger. With Martin here was C. T. Vivian. Vivian had been instrumental in the Nashville movement; he was also one of the Freedom Riders. At this point, he was one of Martin's lieutenants and part of the inner circle of SCLC. I think he is still alive and is continuing church work and movement-related work. I have seen him a few times over the years.

—*Rev. Edwin King, interview by Trent Watts, June 2, 2009, transcript, December 2009, transcript in author's possession.*

The little COFO office on Lynch Street in Jackson that spring hardly looked like the command post for any invasion; although it was not a clandestine operation, it looked more like a small guerilla outpost, deep within some occupied country, waiting for news from the outside world that the invasion had begun. But that outside world was waiting for news from COFO. Most of the summer money arrived at the same time as the summer troops; in late spring SNCC was financing almost everything in COFO. (CORE had a major voter registration campaign, with many arrests, in Madison County in the fourth district that spring and this took most of their money). But SNCC was in one of its destitute periods. For weeks most of the SNCC staff had received only partial paychecks—if any. There was literally not enough money to buy stationary to send out many important mailings, including answering many applications from volunteers who did want to know—in mid-May—if they had been accepted for the summer program. Day by day a little money was found and some emergency business was handled, and some postponed.

—Ed King, "COFO Office," 90. Evans B. Harrington Collection. (MUM00219). Box 14, Folder 9. The Department of Archives and Special Collections, J. D. Williams Library, The University of Mississippi, Oxford, Mississippi.

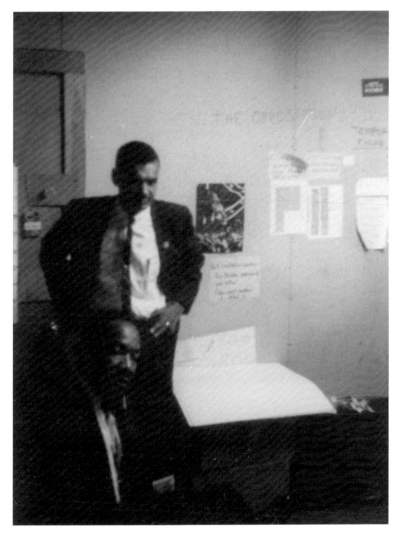

10. Jackson, Miss.—July '64 COFO/SCLC office, M. L. King, C. T. Vivian (Klan poster)

There was constant police surveillance and the constant threat of violence. Hunter Morey, a white SNCC worker from Chicago, had spent most of the year in the Delta, but he was now assigned to the Jackson office to coordinate COFO legal activities for the summer project. He was arrested three times in one day for minor charges. The police probably both wanted information and to harass the staff; they got no information but the harassment did not make his work any easier. The front window to the office was broken out with bricks (and then was boarded up). Somehow the police were never looking when a carload of white hoodlums passed. But if a movement car stopped in the street in front of the office to let someone out, everyone present might get a traffic ticket—or be taken straight to jail. Another white worker, Dick Jewett, a CORE staff man from New York who had spent most of the year in the Canton voter registration work, was now assigned to the Jackson COFO office for summer planning. A tall man with reddish hair, he was always easily recognized by the police. Late in May he was arrested on some false charges and refused to give the police the information they wanted; while in jail he was very badly beaten. This background violence and tension just added to the pressure of time and poverty and the general confusion in the office. But the necessary work somehow got done.

I went into the COFO office almost every afternoon during that May. But I got busy with final exam time on campus and did not go to the office for several days. When I finally did go in I found about eight people working hard on some mailing. Somehow I found out that none of them had eaten at all that day and most of them nothing but sardine sandwiches for the past few days. I gave them what cash I had, about five dollars, to go get some food. But Lois Chafee suggested that they spend most of the money on stamps, another item that had just been exhausted. The others agreed. I gave the money to Bob Moses and he left for a nearby grocery and soon returned with a loaf of bread and a large jar of peanut butter. Everyone was back working at their desks (or makeshift desks) or telephones. Bob walked quietly around the office handing out the bread and letting each person dip a large spoon of peanut butter. I noticed that Bob took no peanut butter himself. He offered me the bread and I did take one piece, for I did need to share this with them all. There was no wine, just water. And the invasion plans continued. We talked about confusion, and violence, and fear, and revolution, but very quietly, in peace. There was something beautiful in these last days of our movement.

—Ed King, "COFO Office," 91–92. Evans B. Harrington Collection. (MUM00219). Box 14, Folder 9. The Department of Archives and Special Collections, J. D. Williams Library, The University of Mississippi, Oxford, Mississippi.

11. Jackson, Miss., July '64, COFO office, SCLC tour, [Ralph] Abernathy, MLK, Annelle Ponder, Miss. SCLC staff

Violence and death were expected by the COFO staff. Because of the obvious situation in Neshoba, we decided there could be no work there in the first part of the summer. In fact, there was no such open work for two full months. A similar area where major violence was certain was the area we called "Southwest," the region below Jackson and Vicksburg along the Mississippi River and north of the Louisiana border. The largest towns here were Natchez and McComb.

The Southwest was the area where SNCC and Bob Moses first began their voter registration work in Mississippi under the initiative of Amzie Moore up in the Delta and the crucial local leadership of C. C. Bryant, both longtime NAACP men. This first SNCC campaign was ended by violence in 1961 with the murder of Herbert Lee. SNCC was forced to abandon the Southwest and retreat to Jackson, and, later, start work in the Delta. There were additional murders in Southwest in the first part of 1964. By early spring crosses were burning; churches were burning. COFO was determined to have a project in Southwest. But in the first few days after Neshoba it was decided to postpone projects in both areas, and when Southwest was opened, to use only old staff persons, no new volunteers. People were expected to die in Southwest. Those who had planned the summer project would go there, leaving the new volunteers in "safer" areas. This decision was announced to the press on July 1 by Bob Moses. The Jackson press played it up as a great defeat for COFO, and consequently, a victory for the methods of the Klan.

COFO had to reconsider the timing of the project when we saw how our decision was being interpreted. There were many local black people (like C. C. Bryant and Mrs. Alynn Quinn) who wanted help with voter registration and Freedom Schools, who wanted to be part of the movement sweeping their state. The violence already existed in Southwest. It would not be brought by the COFO workers. Not to come would be to deny an appeal of the local people (and so deny our own teachings about responding to the grass roots as well as leading the people); worse, it might be understood by local people as a kind of abandonment. Because violence was so bad there, some local blacks might think that even SNCC would not dare help them. And, on the other side, the Klan tactics would look so successful that violence and terrorism would sweep all over the state. If the movement could not face violence in Southwest, we could soon expect major violence in a moderate place like Greenville. And, finally, our commitment to nonviolence looked very shallow if it was valid only in safe, moderate communities. COFO decided to open a project in McComb as early as possible in July.

—*Ed King, "Return to McComb," 32–34. Unpublished manuscript in author's possession.*

12. Jackson, Miss.—July '64, COFO office, Bob Weil

I had important things to do for MFDP in Jackson the day the first group moved into Southwest. A group of congressmen (William Fitz Ryan of New York and Philip Burton, Augustus Hawkins, and Don Edwards, all of California) supporting the MFDP was touring the state. I had to meet with them; several stayed overnight in our home at Tougaloo. They had been given FBI protection everywhere they went. In McComb that same day ten COFO workers moved into a rented brick home . . . The second day I was able to go to McComb . . . Don Edwards . . . learned of my concern for McComb and my planned visit. He asked to come with me. I again explained the danger. He still wanted to come. His son,

Len, a law student, was working on the summer project in Greenwood. The other congressmen returned to Washington.

Don Edwards and I drove to Southwest. The FBI gave us no protection and we did not ask for it. Edwards knew that his earlier treatment had been special. He insisted that I not notify the government that he had stayed on in Mississippi. With only white men in the car, we thought we might not attract any attention. We stopped at a service station for gas in the white section of McComb. The attendants had just finished marking numerals on the restroom doors. They joked with us that the new civil rights law passed by that terrible Congress in Washington made them take down the "white only" sign but if we needed a restroom we were clearly first-rate people and could use "number one" . . . The congressman allowed as to how their sign painting endeavor was certainly very interesting.

Late that evening Don Edwards placed a phone call to a high Justice Department official. The man in Washington, at first, did not believe the congressman was actually still in Mississippi, much less in McComb. Edwards had to tell Washington that he was not joking. At that the crowd of us standing around the phone did laugh. Edwards explained that the noise was from the COFO staff. Washington became quite upset and warned Edwards that there might be serious violence in McComb, that he was in a dangerous situation. The good congressman became furious and used some strong language to tell Washington that if the Justice Department had reason to fear violence in McComb then they should be protecting the civil rights workers. He said that he would spend the night in the [COFO] house and expected to be treated as any civil rights worker. He strongly suggested that congressmen should not be given special protection by the Justice Department when they toured Mississippi. He said he wanted Washington to treat him just as they would the other American citizens in the state working for civil rights. Washington urged him to leave the Freedom House. He refused. So the conversation ended. A few minutes later we received telephone calls from the local police chief, the mayor, and the sheriff. All spoke to the congressman . . . The Freedom House was not bombed that night.*

—Ed King, "Return to McComb," 34–37. Unpublished manuscript in author's possession.

---

* The initial group of eight SNCC workers arrived in McComb on Sunday, July 5, moving into a house at 702 Wall Street owned by Mrs. Willie Mae Cotton. Congressman Don Edwards and Rev. Ed King visited McComb on Monday, July 6. While the house was indeed not bombed that night, in the early hours of July 8 eight sticks of dynamite blew a wall off the house. While no one was killed, project director Curtis Hayes and volunteer Dennis Sweeney were injured. See John Dittmer, *Local People: The Struggle for Civil Rights in Mississippi* (Urbana and Chicago: University of Illinois Press, 1994), 267. See also Bruce Watson, *Freedom Summer: The Savage Season That Made Mississippi Burn and Made America a Democracy* (New York: Viking, 2010), 135-36. For a driving tour of places significant in the McComb civil rights movement, see http://www.winterinstitute.org/documents/McCombDrivingTour.pdf; accessed 1 May 2011.

13. July '64, G'wood Miss. Airport, SCLC tour for the MFDP, Dewey Green's father—Leflore Co. Abernathy, M. L. King, Andy Young, SNCC photographer, C. T. Vivian, Len Edwards, a summer volunteer

Our mood at the beginning of the summer of 1964 was hopeful, but by late July we probably had had maybe as many as ten bombings. We had a church bombed every week and usually one or two other places: homes or meeting sites. But we felt very confident that the local people had responded; they were standing up. It is their movement that we are helping and we have a confident feeling that the nation is responding because of the coverage of the tragedy. But we did feel that the rest of America was with us. At that point, most movement people were very optimistic that when we were to have a national showdown at the Democratic convention over the seating of the MFDP's slate of delegates, the mood of the country would help us to win. I was always a little more cautious. On a stage that big we didn't know what might happen.

The work in the summer of 1964 was designed to get national public opinion really working to help the nation understand the significance of voting and the significance of being denied the right to vote. Throughout the summer we actually thought that the congressional challenge would be more significant than voter registration itself in winning the right to vote for black Mississippians. And this was something we had talked about since the Freedom Vote. The congressional challenge was to have local people run for office for U.S. Congress and then to use the Reconstruction laws we found out through research were still in the statutes. If intimidation of black voters had occurred, under those laws you could have special elections under federal supervision by act of Congress. We actually thought that that challenge was going to be more important than the convention challenge. We thought that we would use the Atlantic City convention as a stage for rallying support. Then we would come back through September and October working on the congressional election.

We were working to bring pressure on the White House in Washington. And Washington was constantly saying they don't have legal authority. We were trying to show that they did. They had legal authority if Americans were being killed and if there was a breakdown in local law, but taking such an action would have taken enormous courage from Washington. But we were building the challenge and anticipated the actual voting using the Reconstruction-era laws and we actually began planning for this campaign all year—well before Atlantic City. Mrs. Hamer and Mrs. Gray and Mrs. Devine tried to run in the Democratic primaries three weeks before Neshoba. I think it was about like today—June 2nd or something like that. And even without the outside volunteers, we had started on this effort, and some of our people said why bother with something like a convention. That's not for real, but Congress is. So, there were some people saying let's just do the November thing. Allard Lowenstein, on the other hand, was the one who had suggested that a focus on the convention—the press coverage of the convention—could help build support for the congressional challenge. With that challenge, we were going to show how much of the Reconstruction law was there that Congress and the president could move on. I was certain that the congressional challenge was real. Some people had criticized the mock vote in the Freedom Vote in 1963 on the grounds that it was not "real." Why risk your life, they asked, for something that is not real? Well, we could understand that argument theoretically, but we believed that the Freedom Vote was a practical and necessary step.

—Rev. Edwin King, interview by Trent Watts, June 2, 2009, transcript, December 2009, transcript in author's possession.

14. G'wood Airport, July 1964, SCLC tour for MFDP, Mr. Green, Abernathy, MLK, Andy Young, John Lewis—SNCC

We certainly understood . . . that the black ministers in the state were going to be against [the movement] if they were not called leaders. But most of the black ministers did not become involved. As late as the time of Martin's death in 1968, Dr. King could not have preached in any white church except First Unitarian Church in Jackson and that church even had a few black members. But I would say at the time of his death, 75 to 80 percent of the black congregations in Mississippi also would not have let Dr. King even into their pulpit. They've got pictures of him now and they would deny that, just like SNCC militant people like to deny how much Jesus talk they used and how much it meant to them to be able to use it. Most of the church was not with the voter registration effort or other aspects of the movement that summer; most of the church was a drag. Fannie Lou Hamer would all but threaten violence on the ministers to get them involved.

The leadership in the black civil rights movement I would say was disproportionately Methodist, certainly was heavily Protestant; that is obvious. The very top leaders like Martin may have been Baptist, but there was sharp disagreement and splits within the black Baptist denominations over the wisdom of direct civil rights activity. But in most of the communities that I know about, the key people who were ready first to take action were black Methodist women. And the Methodist church had a tradition in this country of social concerns, but also a deeper tradition that a born-again life was a life of citizenship as well as a life of salvation. And you just didn't make those distinctions. In fact, in Mississippi Bishop Charles Golden of the black Methodist Church gave out orders in 1963 that black Methodist churches were to be open to Medgar Evers for rallies and were to be open anywhere in the state for SNCC to use.

There were no other available buildings. The public schools are controlled by whites. You could not meet in a public school, you can't go rent a hall in a hotel. The church is the only place that literally had space. No, the bishop didn't say Sunday morning or the communion service or the Good Friday service is going to be [a] civil rights meeting, but he said, "This space," which is controlled by black people, "will be open for voter registration work." There was no other place.

So in most communities there was a little pressure from a church hierarchy, when you went to a local minister that his bishop, who might be five hundred miles away, has still said that even if he didn't join the movement he had to let his church do it. If his church did it, he knew he would be targeted by the white community.

—Rev. Ed King, "Religion and the Civil Rights Movement" (lecture, University of Virginia, Bonhoeffer House, Charlottesville, Virginia, February 27, 2002, http://www.livedtheology.org/pdfs/e_king.pdf; accessed March 29, 2011).

15. July '64, G'wood, Miss., SCLC tour for MFDP, Dick Frey

This is Dick Frey and others at the Methodist Church in Greenwood. This would have been the trip with Dr. King. So this is just a candid shot of some of the student workers. Now Dick had been there all year with SNCC. Early in the summer Stokely Carmichael was head of the Greenwood project. Then I think Bob Zellner may have become head there and Stokely may have sort of been coordinating things for the district. It's odd I don't have Stokely popped up in one of those pictures.

—*Rev. Edwin King, interview by Trent Watts, June 2, 2009, transcript, December 2009, transcript in author's possession.*

The movement in Mississippi had already used a "mock" election in the Freedom Vote to both educate black people about politics and to demonstrate the denial of the right to vote. The basic plan for the 1964 Freedom Summer was to have a "mock" organizing campaign for the right to organize. In the summer we would use the instruments—Freedom Schools, adult community centers, research projects, voter registration, a political party, even a white community project among the poor and workers—that we hoped to be free to use during the next decade, starting in the fall of 1964 when the "real" organizing might begin—with some small but sure sign that harassment could not totally break us: that voter registration and political organization efforts were not folly.

There was a time when time itself was not seen as working against the possibilities of freedom in America. SNCC, then, thought that change was still possible and might have been able to wait for a while. That much SNCC had learned from the "grassroots" people in Mississippi, from the earth. But new lessons were learned in the failures of the federal government in the summer of 1964 and old hopes died. Perhaps such a long-range perspective on time was really "un-American." In the final intensity of Freedom Summer most SNCC men and women became very American, very frustrated, very bitter, very angry, and, it seems, even too exhausted to learn the new meaning of time necessary for those who know the only hope is revolution.

Most of the white volunteers of the 1964 Freedom Summer came South to "save Mississippi" and to "help the poor black folks." The police state formalities and the violence of the Klan was also seen as necessary to "save our way of life." The liberal administration in Washington did not act responsibly or intervene, perhaps out of political expediency to save itself, perhaps because there was some kind of recognition that the movement had to be stopped in order to save the "powers that be" in America. SNCC and COFO just want to "save the movement" so we could finally begin to organize the people. Rita Schwerner understood that we now had "to get a nasty job done." In 1963 and in the spring of 1964 we knew it had to be done in Mississippi—and we thought it could be done there first, then there would be time to work on all our problems—in Mississippi and in the rest of America. By the end of the Freedom Summer we had learned things many of us would have preferred not to know—now we had to get a nasty job done—in America.

—Ed King, "Needles and Spears," 88–89. Evans B. Harrington Collection. (MUM00219). Box 14, Folder 9. The Department of Archives and Special Collections, J. D. Williams Library, The University of Mississippi, Oxford, Mississippi.

16. M. L. King, Ralph Abernathy, B. Lafayette, Neshoba Co., Phil., Miss., July, 1964

Here we've got Martin Luther King, Ralph Abernathy, and Bernard Lafayette; this is still in July 1964. Around this time we actually had a summit meeting on the Tougaloo College campus using a room in the student union. Later in the morning somebody else needed it, so we ended up meeting at my house. We were discussing what would go on at the Atlantic City convention. Andrew Young was there. Bayard Rustin was with us at that meeting at my house. CORE would have been represented. As I said, the national NAACP was absolutely not part of what we were doing and would not have participated. Martin was here for several days. He went up into the Delta to Greenwood before we went to Neshoba. He went to Vicksburg. I didn't go on the Vicksburg trip because I still had family members there and people understood that I wasn't going to do anything or risk anything public in Vicksburg. I believe that Martin made those trips before we went up to Neshoba.

The primary purpose of Martin's trip to Neshoba County was to support the MFDP and to support the Freedom Summer workers. It was to show people in Neshoba that he will stand with them. Mississippi was arguably the hardest place in America; those are the people suffering the most. So, he is saying that he will be with them for a few hours, but that he is not afraid. He used the events in the town of Philadelphia, though, for voter registration. He went door to door, up and down the street. This is in the part of Philadelphia called Freedom Quarters, a black side of town across the railroad and up a little hill. And he told people you need to register to vote and the first step is registering to vote in the Freedom Democratic Party. And we had staff people going along and explaining that we were going to go to the national convention—this sort of thing. With visits to local churches in other places we would have explained what things like political parties and delegates and conventions were over three different nights because people couldn't imagine. There in Philadelphia with Martin it was speeded up because this was our first foray in with him.

I had met Abernathy in 1960. I was arrested with him in Montgomery. I had met Martin in Montgomery in 1958. I didn't meet Abernathy on that trip. I just went to Martin's church and then to his home. The number of people in the civil rights movement at any one time was probably never more than one thousand and that Freedom Summer of 1964 would have been the highest to that point. Then with the Selma march a year later the movement would have again about a thousand people actively involved. Most of the time SNCC would have been less than one hundred people and the others were small as well. My point is simply that people in the movement knew each other regardless of organizational affiliation.

I thought these men worked as a perfect team. Each knew the other's talents, but there generally would be a two-way split as they spoke to a crowd. Ralph would do it, but [Bernard] Lafayette or others could have. Usually Ralph would work the crowd with the more traditional preacher style and get the whoops and the hollers and the amens going and then get a response going and then Martin would come in and things would be quieter, more philosophic, more theological, even. Martin certainly could have used the more traditional style. He does use the call and response as a liturgical speaking device. But I thought that Ralph and the other more traditional speakers were always underestimated with average black church audiences. Martin's talk was what mainline white America could relate to and so could educated blacks. These other men freed him from having to do that. Had he done, and I'm not being pejorative when I'm talking about these things, had he done some of that style—Charles Evers did it frequently—the media would have focused on the sound bites of the cheers and the crowds, not the substantive things that Martin could get in.

—Rev. Edwin King, interview by Trent Watts, June 2, 2009, transcript, December 2009, transcript in author's possession.

17. Leflore [Co.], Greenwood, Miss., July, 1964, SCLC tour for MFDP, Andy Young, Willie Peacock

ndrew Young was in on the discussions of our strategy for the Atlantic City Democratic National Convention. I don't remember him saying much, but he was certainly there in the meetings at Tougaloo College at my house. He is regarded by this point—this is a year after the Birmingham campaign—he is regarded as very close to Dr. King and a very important part of anything that goes on—just part of the inner circle. I had met him several times. During the 1963 Jackson campaign, Dr. Dan Beittel, the president of Tougaloo College, Memphis Norman, who was a student at Tougaloo, and Andrew, and I all spoke at Broadway Tabernacle Congregational Church in New York City. That was the first time I had talked with him in much detail. He was talking about the Birmingham campaign; we were talking about the Jackson campaign. Even then you understood that you wanted him to agree with your ideas because Martin respects his opinions.

—*Rev. Edwin King, interview by Trent Watts, June 2, 2009, transcript, December 2009, transcript in author's possession.*

One of the things we wanted to do in the 1964 summer was to break the back of the violent resistance in the state, to do it by offering ourselves nonviolently in the face of it, to absorb as much of the suffering as we could. We had seen for several years that we had absorbed just about as much as we with the grace of God could endure. We couldn't see that any more of us dying was going to do anything. We could not get the national press's attention to the violence going on down here or the repression or the failures of the national government to act on the collapse of the police force or anything else. There were occasional stories in the national news, but very little compared to what was going on daily here.

—*Rev. R. Edwin King, Jr., interview by John Jones, November 8, 1980, transcript, July, 1982, 108, Mississippi Department of Archives and History, Jackson, Mississippi.*

Tactically [and] strategically what we had to do within the movement would be called consciousness-raising now. We had to get the oppressed people to change their identity of themselves. They had to stand up and claim their freedom and claim their dignity. And this was done over and over in the sense of you are already a child of God, you are born again in this sense, you can now claim who you are in the eyes of God . . . They were called upon to stand up for what was inside them, that the blood of Jesus had been shed for them and they could stand up. And that was the starting point for their identity. And then to stand up and fight the system, and when you stood up you also had to hold up your brothers and sisters who were suffering. Hold on to each other, hold up each other, and everybody stand up . . . We also had to . . . let America, the rest of the nation, know that black people weren't just waiting to be saved by Washington. That they were standing up demanding. Now, that shocked America . . . We appealed first to Washington, to the liberals in the White House, the Kennedys and Johnsons and found out that they weren't going to help us . . . We had to make the whole American system work, and the civil rights movement did that in a beautiful way, rallying all kinds of people.

—*Rev. Ed King, "Religion and the Civil Rights Movement" (lecture, University of Virginia, Bonhoeffer House, Charlottesville, Virginia, February 27, 2002, http://www.livedtheology.org/pdfs/e_king.pdf; accessed March 29, 2011).*

18. Pool Hall—Listening to M. L. King, Neshoba, Phil., Miss., July, 1964

My major work that summer was with the Mississippi Freedom Democratic Party. I visited many of the local projects in all parts of the state. For the MFDP I accompanied Dr. Martin Luther King and the SCLC party on their five-day tour of the state. Dr. King spoke at rallies promoting the MFDP . . . The most interesting part of this week . . . was the visit to Neshoba County. COFO had asked me to be the official MFDP host for Martin Luther King on what I regarded as a trip through Hell.

—*Ed King, "Testimony From Mt. Zion," 1. Unpublished manuscript in author's possession.*

In the photo here it is summer, of course, and the kids are out of school wandering around; they are thrilled by the excitement King's visit represented. The fact that the crowd is so young also means some of the adults are peeping out the window. While we didn't get as many adults in the crowd as we wanted, we were quite glad to have the kids. They certainly would have known who Dr. King was. I mean this is a year after the Birmingham campaign and eleven months after the march on Washington. And the word quickly spread—did you hear that's Dr.

King down the street? But they would have never heard of the Freedom Democratic Party. In this picture he would have talked again about the right to vote and how it's theirs. But he also told them that the right is meaningless if you don't try to do it. He said that we want people in Neshoba County to take the voter registration test at the courthouse, but until we are ready for that we want you to sign up for the FDP. We have sheets, he would have said, for those who are old enough. Like any political leader, he would have repeated the same things over and over. We had with us the freedom registration forms, as well as copies of the regular state form that we would use in workshops to teach them how to take the test, but we also had a legal-size document that we would let them sign.

I'm sure half of them said, "Well, come on, that can't be Dr. King," and the other kids said, "Yes it is, let's go." And some of the parents said, "Don't you dare go," and the kids came.

We were working with the kids in Freedom Schools where we were active in the state that summer because we anticipated public school integration was coming, and we wanted to try to prepare them for that as best we could. There was only token integration that fall, but the prospect of school integration had been another major force in bringing things to a head that summer. We had talked about the issue through the winter and wondered if kids would be killed when the first grade was integrated. We asked, "Won't the white South fight harder than at Ole Miss?" "No," we said, "not if we bring everything to a head and nonviolently show that we will bear the suffering." We talked this way. We said, "If we can bear several months of this, then September with the schools may not be the crisis Meredith was." Cynically we said, "We've got to prepare those kids academically for school integration, so we've got to teach them math and English," and we expanded that to black history, and then theatre and art and music and all kinds of wonderful things with the Freedom Schools. But just as important, we wanted the kids at the Freedom Schools to be so happy with what they were doing that the parents would come back at night to an adult school on the meaning of citizenship. So we were using the kids in a positive way.

—*Rev. Edwin King, interview by Trent Watts, June 2, 2009, transcript, December 2009, transcript in author's possession.*

19. SCLC Tour for MFDP, M. L. King and Co. approach Pool Hall, Philadelphia, Neshoba Co., Miss., July, 1964

Here are Andrew Young and Martin Luther King leading a group down the street in Philadelphia. The black churches in Philadelphia simply would not or could not have hosted us. They were not ready yet. Soon they opened up to organizing efforts, I think, through the fall of 1964, and they began to host meetings. At this point, however, had we been able to hold a rally in a church, we would have. In fact there were some churches up there in that section of town and in later years those churches were centers of movement activity. We certainly would have used a church rather than the pool hall and Martin would have gone to the pool hall afterwards. The crowd would have gathered spontaneously, but we would have had people handing out leaflets and things like that on the edges. And the people would have been invited to come hear Dr. King speak. Come meet Dr. King, they were told. Why is he in Philadelphia? Well, he cares about the missing men and he cares about voter registration. And he is helping organize the Freedom Democratic Party. It would have been the same line as in the visit to Greenwood.

—Rev. Edwin King, interview by Trent Watts, June 2, 2009, transcript, December 2009, transcript in author's possession.

Neshoba was a county with great poverty for all races. The red clay hills and swamps held only small farms, no plantations; timber was the major source of income. The black population was low, less than 20 percent, although nearby counties were plantation and cotton areas with high black populations … Unlike the natural beauty of much of Mississippi, Neshoba had a raw, lean, hungry, ugly look, like a mangy, starving wolf.

—Ed King, "Neshoba," 3. Unpublished manuscript in author's possession.

We had surprising protection if not hospitality. We had a motorcade of several COFO cars, reporters, FBI agents, and state police. In Neshoba the FBI gave extensive protection to Dr. King. Again, their protestations that this was not their job were proved ridiculous; this was their job when it was politically appropriate. Only black citizens and white civil rights workers who were not so famous were refused protection. As we drove through the pines and came into the red hills of Neshoba we could see cars and men blocking the dirt roads to our sides. Some were probably state highway patrol officers; others may have been deputies. We trusted none of them, but they seemed under some plan and instructions. In the little town of Philadelphia we passed the huge lumber mills and railroad tracks and then went up into the small hills of the Independence Quarters, the isolated black section of town.

Among those with us for this trip were more ministers from SCLC: Andy Young, C. T. Vivian, and Ralph Abernathy, my old friend from Montgomery, with whom I was having lunch way back in 1960 when we were arrested. It was my first arrest, but not so for the veteran Abernathy. By 1964 we both had long records. The SNCC chairman, John Lewis, with an arrest record longer than both of us, was also present. All these men made comments to the small and cautious [group of] blacks who joined us, but the major attention was on Dr. King.

—Ed King, "Testimony From Mt. Zion," 1–2. Unpublished manuscript in author's possession.

The Jackson television and national television probably came. We had a media office. We would have alerted both SCLC in Atlanta and local people. But with Dr. King here aiming at national attention, I've seen so many cameras that I don't remember, but we certainly would have asked the media to come. We had a caravan of cars. We wanted to have people to hand out literature so we had some workers there. By that time there was so much national attention on the state.

—Rev. Edwin King, interview by Trent Watts, June 2, 2009, transcript, December 2009, transcript in author's possession.

The truth about the federal response to Freedom Summer is more complex than we in the civil rights movement imagined in 1964 and is not yet known. The president expected an outbreak of terrible violence in Mississippi. This was not a matter of if there would be violence, but of when and where the first incident would occur. In 2001 in my research in the presidential papers in the Johnson Library I found an amazing and appalling document in which President Johnson recognizes the certainty of violence and wants all agencies of the federal government to be prepared to respond. This is a one-page memo reprinted here.

June 17, 1964

MEMORANDUM FOR
    Burke Marshall
    Assistant Attorney General
    Department of Justice

    The President is aware that he will be faced with questions concerning the Mississippi voter registration program and has asked for adequate information with which to respond. I would appreciate it therefore if we could have at your earliest convenience replies to the following questions plus any additional information you believe bears on the problem:

    1. Under what conditions can Federal marshals or Federal troops be sent to Mississippi to protect the college students from bodily harm or harassment?

    2. What has the Justice Department, the FBI, or the entire Federal government done so far by way of preparing for what appears to be a highly explosive situation?

    3. What additional steps are contemplated?

    4. Have all of the necessary preliminary actions been thought through so that at the very first outbreak of difficulties the President will be prepared to act?

    5. What are the various alternatives that will be available to the Federal government in the event of widespread disorders?

    6. Are there any steps that the President could consider taking between now and the first outbreak of violence?

In my limited research I was unable to determine the author of this memorandum. Note that the date is four days before the June 21, 1964, murder of the three civil rights workers in Neshoba County. It is directed to Burke Marshall in the Department of Justice. In this document President Johnson wants information on possible federal action before the expected "outbreak of violence." But the FBI and the Justice Department failed President Johnson. By the time of the Neshoba murders even President Johnson must have known (or suspected) that "the outbreak of violence" had begun and federal action was needed. The American government failed to protect American citizens.

Note the first sentence of this government document. The federal government properly identifies the Freedom Summer campaign as a "voter registration program" and federal response would be needed. COFO said this before the program began.

Note item 1. The government recognizes it has the power to send in marshals or even troops to protect the college students (the Freedom Summer volunteers). COFO said this same government had the power to also protect black citizens and civil rights workers.

Note item 2. The government recognizes that the start of the 1964 Freedom Summer in Mississippi "appears to be a highly explosive situation."

Note item 3. The government "contemplates" the obvious need for "additional steps."

Note item 4. The government assumes there will be an "outbreak of difficulties" causing the president "to act."

Note item 5. The government recognizes there may be "widespread disorders."

Note item 6. The government and the president assume there will be an "outbreak of violence."

The first "outbreak of violence" began on June 16, 1964, in Neshoba County when the KKK and white police attacked Mt. Zion Methodist Church. Black people were beaten and the church burned. A few days later, on June 19, FBI agents investigated the church burning and interviewed some of these victims. So the FBI knew full well the violence in Mississippi had escalated to a new level. It was the duty of the FBI to inform the Justice Department and the president. Near midnight on June 21 three young Americans, James Chaney, Michael Schwerner, and Andrew Goodman, were murdered.

The American government failed. This memorandum states that "the President is aware." In this particular document President Lyndon Johnson seems wise in his understanding of the Deep South and ready to face the expected violence in some way. But the three men were allowed to be killed. Was this the failure of the FBI to inform the Justice Department, or of the Justice Department to inform the president, or what? Whatever, our government failed, and this was a shock to the Freedom Summer volunteers that started a reevaluation of everything they had been taught and believed about the American system.

—Ed King. *Unpublished manuscript in author's possession. Memo to Burke Marshall, 6/17/64, HU2/ST24/EG135/PL/ST24/HU2–7/ST 24 File, WHCF, LBJ Library.*

20. SCLC/MFDP tour, Philadelphia—Ct. House, Neshoba Co., Miss., July, 1964

Clearly you have a sheriff's department vehicle here. And we were very afraid of the sheriff's department. And it turned out we had every right to be. However, very few white people in Mississippi would have believed that they were associated with the organized violence. We were told that by local black people. So we thought that the sheriff and deputies were involved in the disappearance of the three workers. A kind of logic would say how do people disappear in America in a town and the police can't find any trace? But there would have been no proof at that point.

We would not have stopped there. I think I probably just took that photograph because it was the local police visible. We would not have dared to stop at the courthouse. We would have gotten a parking ticket even if we had used a parking meter.

—Rev. Edwin King, interview by Trent Watts, June 2, 2009, transcript, December 2009, transcript in author's possession.

My wife, Jeannette, and I [had] arrived back at Tougaloo College from the Oxford, Ohio, training camp for summer volunteers on Saturday, June 20, 1964.

On Sunday morning I was the guest preacher [in Jackson] at Farish Street Baptist Church, where the pastor and many members supported the movement. My sermon theme was the old spiritual "Joshua Fought the Battle of Jericho," with the emphasis on the basic goal of Freedom Summer. The children of Israel had to march around the walls of Jericho seven times; their confident enemies mocked them, secure in their fortification. The walls of Jericho reminded me of the wall of racism . . . an all-American wall. None of us in the movement expected to see the wall destroyed. But in Mississippi the movement and the black people were so oppressed that even walking around the wall in a demonstration was blocked by federally upheld injunctions, police dogs, guns, bombs, and worst of all, the internal spiritual fear and hopelessness. If, at the end of Freedom Summer, a handful of us have survived the first walk around these walls, then the movement will have survived in Mississippi and someone will keep on keeping on. This was our daring, desperate, and modest goal. It takes faith for our ragtag army to stand up to the wall; most of us will never see the wall crumble. Most of us will never hear the trumpets blare and the people shout. We do believe that, someday, we (or our children) will overcome.

I did not mention the white men who had tried to attack our house only a few hours earlier that night; that was routine. After church I walked to my car, the well-known white Rambler, and discovered a ticket for an uncommitted traffic offense; that was even more normal. The Jericho Police Department was laughing at us.

—*Ed King, "Neshoba," 2. Unpublished manuscript in author's possession.*

21. Pool Hall—M. L. King plays—then speaks for MFDP, Neshoba Co., Philadelphia, Miss., July 1964

I think the men were very impressed by Martin's presence in the pool hall. Among some local black people, however, a kind of puritanism prevailed—it would not be as strong now, but it existed then—some of them would have been uncomfortable with his being in that kind of place, because they themselves were trying desperately to hold on to a little more secure, respectable lifestyle. His playing pool would only be a few minutes. Then he would start talking and we would be working the back of the crowd with voter registration materials. "Won't you take this?" "Will you take this to your parents?"

—Rev. Edwin King, interview by Trent Watts, June 2, 2009, transcript, December 2009, transcript in author's possession.

Martin spoke of nonviolence, love, and politics. Martin was well aware that many black children had followed him as we walked around and now were staring through the windows into the pool hall. The children and teenagers were his focus in some of his remarks:

"They [the missing men] have probably given their lives for your freedom and mine. I see a lot of young people here. Now you have been born into a world that presents you with so many conditions that cause you to feel that you are inferior, that cause you to feel less than a white man. But if I can leave anything with you this afternoon, I want each of you to feel that you are just as good as anybody else that God created in the world. I want you to know that you are somebody and that you are God's children."

The pool hall scene was anything but jovial for me. We were crowded inside the hot, dark rooms. I was impressed with Martin's words but worried that even a small bomb in that place would kill all of us. Then Martin spoke about fear:

"With all the conditions you live with there is the temptation for you to be afraid. But if we are gonna be free as a people, we've got to shed ourselves of fear and we've got to say to those who oppose us with violence that you can't stop us by bombing a church. You can't stop us by shooting at us. You can't stop us by brutalizing us because we're gonna keep on keeping on until we're free."

—Ed King, "Testimony From Mt. Zion," 2–3. *Unpublished manuscript in author's possession.*

One white evangelist from New Orleans, Rev. Bob Harrington, became quite involved in the Neshoba case. Harrington had built a reputation preaching to strippers and other sinners in the French Quarter where he, so he announced, was known as the "Chaplain of Bourbon Street" . . . The Bourbon Street Chaplain attacked King as a "false prophet, seeking gain for himself and not the Kingdom of God or his own race . . . I challenge Martin Luther King to explain how he calls himself a minister of the gospel when the gospel is the good news of the Lord . . . Some preacher this Martin Luther King is . . . he comes into town and instead of a Bible, he uses a pool stick."

—Ed King, "Neshoba," 22, 23. *Unpublished manuscript in author's possession.*

22. M. L. King in Pool Hall, No Bad Language, Neshoba Co., Phil., Miss., July 1964

O n the very first day of Freedom Summer, three young men were killed: James Chaney, Michael Schwerner, and Andrew Goodman. The fate of those young men was on Martin's mind, on everyone's mind. Chaney and Schwerner were my friends; I had met Goodman at the Ohio "bootcamp." Mickey Schwerner and his wife, Rita, had worked for CORE in Meridian for several months. J. E. Chaney was one of the local people who joined the movement. Andy Goodman was a summer volunteer from Queens College. It was his first day in Mississippi.

That evening I was called by Bob Weil from the Jackson COFO office. Bob told me that three men, Chaney, Goodman, and Schwerner, were missing. They had gone from Meridian into Neshoba County early that afternoon to investigate the burning of Mt. Zion Methodist Church. They had not returned to Meridian on schedule. A carefully worked out procedure for such cases was being followed. Meridian COFO, under the direction of a newly arrived volunteer, Louise Hermey from New Jersey, now working as "Security Officer," made all the checks it could; then Jackson COFO was notified; then the state police and the federal authorities. I was told that every hospital had been checked to see if there had been an accident; more reasonably, every jail in several counties had been checked by telephone. Every response denied any knowledge of the men. We assumed this meant that they were in jail or dead. We assumed that they were in mortal danger if the police officials were lying about holding them. I had absolute confidence in Bob Weil and the COFO office staff. They would do all that could be done.

The proper things were done by the COFO staff; the proper things were not done by the government of the United States. The men were murdered.

The story of the Neshoba martyrs became a key movement myth over the next days, weeks, and years as details emerged. The three men had returned from the Ohio training camp to the Meridian base. Schwerner and Chaney had been organizing in Neshoba County, thirty miles away... Mickey Schwerner had been noticed by the police and most local whites, including the Klan, for several months. His goatee made him quite visible. With his wife, Rita, living inside the black community of Meridian, their visibility and the white anger increased. His Jewish name let the Klan merge anti-Semitism with racism. Stories later came out from paid informants in the Klan that Mickey Schwerner's execution had become a goal... When the Klan had attacked the carload of us from Tougaloo in nearby Madison County three weeks earlier, it is likely that some of the Neshoba Klan men were involved, possibly the deputy sheriff who had volunteered to help control voting demonstrators in Canton. That night the white men had clearly said that they planned murder as one way to stop the invaders in the Freedom Summer, and had a nearby place ready to use. I told the volunteers in Ohio how we escaped by talking to the white men. Chaney, Goodman, and Schwerner knew that story. They did not escape.

—Ed King, "Neshoba," 1, 2–3, 4–5. Unpublished manuscript in author's possession.

In midweek after the disappearance of the three civil rights workers I received a strange message from Neshoba—their bodies were buried beneath a new dam. A black woman who worked at Tougaloo College came to me with the report. She carefully explained that a white woman in Neshoba had given this information to a sister of the lady at Tougaloo to pass on to me—specifically, that I might inform the FBI. The information was sent directly to me, but with the provision that I was to make no effort to discover the identity of the white lady in Neshoba County. A further requirement was that I must never reveal to the FBI the identities of the three ladies involved in this chain of communication. The black woman and the white woman in Neshoba had sufficient reason to be fearful; the black woman also needed protection. I agreed to these provisions before I was given the information. I thought all was quite reasonable.

In the Mississippi movement we had learned that it could be dangerous to use names around the FBI. Earlier that winter, Lewis Allen, key witness to the 1961 murder of Herbert Lee in Amite County in the initial SNCC voter registration campaign, had himself been murdered in Wilkinson County. In COFO we were convinced that this was because Allen had talked to the FBI, who, we heard, had mentioned this accusation of murder against a white man to the local white sheriff. Perhaps this was just routine FBI procedure to check the reputation of the black man for veracity. Whites found out and killed Lewis Allen.

In the Neshoba case, as in any important matter, we could not give the names of local contacts to the FBI without permission. I phoned the FBI, who now had agents in Jackson. I told them that I had some information on the missing men in Neshoba. Two FBI agents came out to Tougaloo College to talk with me. I gave them the message that the bodies of the three missing men were now buried under a new dam. I carefully explained my sources and why I could not give identification information on the women. I could not assure the FBI that this information was not just another rumor. They questioned me further. I could say that this new dam was in Neshoba County; I could not say where it was. I told them that the only dam-like construction that I knew about was earthwork that was part of the new Ross Barnett Reservoir on the Pearl River between Jackson and Neshoba County or highway construction near Meridian. The agents wanted to know where I thought this dam really was. I told them it must be close to Neshoba, where the men disappeared, for the killers to begin burial of the bodies that night—probably in Mississippi, but perhaps in nearby Alabama. I told them I could possibly learn more, and that the white woman wanted to send information to the FBI, but only through me. I knew that she was willing to continue risking her life. I explained that she was willing to serve as a continuing source. The FBI would not accept this chain of information.

I was questioned—practically harassed—about this matter. Agents visited me several times demanding to know the name of the woman at Tougaloo College who was part of the link to Neshoba County. They understood that this was the only name that I did know—if they accepted my story, that is. The FBI insisted that they be allowed to interview her. I assured them that she knew nothing that she had not told me except, perhaps, the name of the white woman who was the key information source. I refused to give the name; the FBI agents became quite angry.

I was contacted once by some young northern FBI agents who had just been sent to Mississippi. They were surprisingly polite and genuinely concerned about the problems of civil rights. They found it hard to accept that I was convinced that the FBI could not be trusted and that I agreed with the three women on this point. My statements seemed to hurt them in a very deep personal way. They were better than an earlier agent who had muttered remarks hinting that I must be a Communist if I would not help the FBI.

I did have my own thoughts about all this. I knew the two women from Neshoba were risking their lives. I knew it took great courage for the black woman who worked in the cafeteria at the college to become involved at all. I thought the white woman in Neshoba might actually know names of white men in the case—perhaps men in her own family. I wondered if the black woman link in this chain might work for the white woman. I admired their courage and American patriotism and sense of duty. I did wonder if this woman was in the Methodist Church and might have known about me as a Methodist minister. Some years later I asked my white friend Florence Mars, active in the Philadelphia Methodist Church, about this connection. Florence assured me that she herself was not this woman and did not know who it might be. So this good mystery woman could be any woman. After the first few days, the FBI never contacted me again about the matter, not even six weeks later, when the bodies of James Chaney, Andrew Goodman, and Michael Schwerner were discovered in a farm dam under construction in Neshoba County.

—Ed King. Unpublished manuscript in author's possession.

23. M. L. King speaks in Pool Hall for MFDP, Neshoba Co., Philadelphia, Miss., July 1964

Here in the photo with King would be SCLC staff. It is hard to tell, but I think that is Bernard [Lafayette]. Now, I'm not sure, but it is certainly an SCLC person. Also, a CORE guy who went along coordinating work like that was Matteo Suarez, out of New Orleans. He was based in Canton, which was the headquarters for that congressional district.

Probably a third of the CORE people were not native Mississippians and two-thirds were. Even more than the local people, the nonnatives would have appreciated the danger of the place because the local people would have probably thought I can find a way to get out of this if it gets really wild. There will be somebody on the block to hide us. The people from Atlanta or Washington, D.C., or places like that would have if anything been more insecure because they had come to this hellhole where people disappeared.

Mississippi was the symbol of the worst and as long as it could survive, the white South could think we can always go back. If Mississippi can hold on, then Alabama can and then we can spread and hold the line. And that's why standing up to violence was essential; you either had to stand up to it with self defense or with non-violence. I mean the rationale of Washington was simply to leave Mississippi alone because it's too dangerous.

—Rev. Edwin King, interview by Trent Watts, June 2, 2009, transcript, December 2009, transcript in author's possession.

I think nonviolence did work...I think it has to do with the fact that the black community and the whites who helped the black community believed in nonviolence in the face of any enemy and lived it so long and beyond that they really believed in Christian love and forgiveness. It was hard: you laughed, you hated, you feared, and you still tried to love your enemy. People always talked about what will be here when we finish. It is not what we do, it is what we are building. Therefore, how we do it is the important thing. That's why what you built up in the spirit of the people was so important. That's why nonviolence fit a grassroots democratic movement rather than an autocratic kind of thing or a thing run by experts. I think it's a great example of a successful nonviolent movement. We certainly haven't solved all our problems, but we are more able as black and white Mississippians to solve them than we ever would have been if there had been the kind of reasonable human, black retaliation and violence first in self-defense and secondarily guerilla violence and terrorism back . . . But we didn't use fear. The discipline and the idea of nonviolence . . . stuck to people; [they] kept using it, even when they would practice self-defense at home. I knew that people were arming themselves once the wave of church bombing began and it started in June, maybe late May, but certainly by June with Mt. Zion being bombed in Neshoba County . . . We knew that was going to escalate. Those bombings went on for sixty to sixty-five weeks [with] at least one bombing a week, then it began to dribble out to one bombing every two or three weeks. That's a long time to wait for moderates to move or the federal government to act.

—*Rev. R. Edwin King, Jr., interview by John Jones, November 8, 1980, transcript, July, 1982, 114–115, Mississippi Department of Archives and History, Jackson, Mississippi.*

24. Confed. statue/Ct. House, SCLC tour, Neshoba Co., Phil., Miss., July, 1964

Here is the Neshoba County Courthouse, with the Confederate statue which recently has been discreetly moved. The moving of the statue is a different problem; I do not like to rewrite history. I think we need to recognize why a statue was there, who put it up, and what it meant to them. I try to find some value in it.

Our goal was to eventually get people to go to that courthouse to take the voter registration test. And what do they have to go do? They have to pass the

Confederate statue, pass police who are around it, pass the deputies who run their lives. The challenge was tremendous, because the atmosphere was so deliberately threatening.

—*Rev. Edwin King, interview by Trent Watts, June 2, 2009, transcript, December 2009, transcript in author's possession.*

The police state atmosphere was there long before you have the 1960s [and] blacks being illegally thrown into prison and beaten and killed and all of that but there was no decent white middle-class morality left to resist the Klan when the Klan finally came along. The white middle class—I don't mean to imply that other people are not moral—I was talking in sociological terms—the kind of people who should have prevented Neshoba and all the rest had been wiped out in the 1950s and silenced and eventually wiped out . . . I know of three friends in the spring of 1958 whose parents were contacted by the Citizens' Council wanting to know why their sons and daughters were going to graduate school in the North and it was advising that it was not wise for their sons and daughters ever to return to Mississippi.

We hesitated to come back to Mississippi because of our families. My wife Jeannette's maiden name was Sylvester; her family lived in Forest Hill, a Jackson suburb. We felt that they might not be attacked or anything because of me or her since she had my name—good old-fashioned chauvinist days—and we came to Tougaloo College, so we thought that they might not suffer but they suffered a good deal out of fear. Not what happened to them directly but they still went through a hell of a lot of worry. With my family it was outright attack. Although they were segregationists. Vicious, massive attacks on them . . . My family was run out of the state . . . in 1960 . . . People stopped speaking to them. Friends that they had known their entire lives. People were afraid to be associated with them. That they might be thought of as supporting me. People would not speak to them in grocery stores. Those who did speak to them insulted them. Basically "why can't you control that Communist?"—this kind of thing. Ministers in the Methodist Church told my parents that the Communists had gained control of me and I was going to a Communist seminary in Boston. That is what pastoral help they got. Finally people stopped shaking hands with my father at church. And would not even speak to my mother at church.

—*Rev. R. Edwin King, Jr., interview by John Jones, November 8, 1980, transcript, July, 1982, 13, 39–40, Mississippi Department of Archives and History, Jackson, Mississippi.*

25. Neshoba Co. Ct. House and segregated public library, Philadelphia, Miss., SCLC tour for MFDP, July, '64

The three bodies [of the missing men] were found by the FBI on August 4. The news was released to the nation late that evening. By the very next day far more important news was shocking the nation; we in Mississippi remained fixed on Neshoba. The president announced that PT boats from North Vietnam had attacked U.S. destroyers in a place called the Gulf of Tonkin. I heard that with disbelief and disgust. I was at the University of Kentucky speaking about Freedom Summer. My distrust of Lyndon Johnson must have seemed paranoid to my hosts. Like most movement people, I opposed the U.S. action in Vietnam. But my response to Lyndon Johnson and Tonkin was not based on any understanding of international politics. I reacted from a Mississippi perspective. I thought that the news was patently absurd, that no one could believe a tiny nation like North Vietnam would have attacked the American navy, that America had most likely attacked North Vietnam and provoked some kind of defensive action if, indeed, any American ships had actually been attacked. I was quite willing to believe that the American navy and the American president would and could lie with ease. But the real reason I doubted the American version of Tonkin was that I thought Lyndon Johnson was using some minor foreign event to deliberately distract American attention from Mississippi and those bodies in Neshoba. My world and time centered on Mississippi.

The government seemed more willing to make a massive response to some unproved "attack" on Americans halfway around the world than to make any significant response to protect the now-proved attack on American citizens inside America. The first duty of any government is to guarantee the rights of its citizens within the nation. My views about Tonkin were shared by many friends. Such an attitude rather obviously shows some paranoia and hubris. The movement had both, but also a most advantageous position from which to see and judge the truth in and about America. A few days later Bob Moses led COFO staff in an informal memorial service for our brothers. Standing in a circle around the ruins of Mt. Zion church Bob made the obvious comparison that the United States government which did not protect freedom here in Neshoba was now attacking Vietnam. This was the first major linking of the civil rights movement and Vietnam. It was no accident that, later, the student rebellion and the major opposition to the war in Vietnam grew out of the Mississippi Freedom Summer.

—Ed King, "Neshoba Fair," 1–2. Unpublished manuscript in author's possession.

26. Ruins of Mt. Zion Church, SCLC tour for the MFDP, Neshoba Co., Miss., July, 1964, R. Abernathy, C. T. Vivian, M. L. King, Dorothy Cotton, Bernard Lafayette, John Lewis

Now, this photograph is taken at Mount Zion Methodist Church. The men disappear on Sunday night the 21st of June; the FBI had been at the church on Friday the 19th of June interviewing people. And parenthetically, the FBI knew that people had been beaten unconscious at that church. The FBI would not respond two days later when we were begging for help and they said they could not intervene because they did not have enough information that there was real trouble. I think the church was probably burned on the preceding Wednesday, which would make it the 16th of June. Word was slowly getting out, but enough word had gotten out. Martin Luther King's trip to Neshoba was a response because the church had been burned, people at the church were attacked, and men were missing.

You also see Dorothy Cotton and John Lewis as well. John Lewis is head of SNCC. Dorothy Cotton kind of holds the office together for SCLC. I would not call her a secretary, but I do not know what her title was. She also helped recruit people for the training programs. But she is sort of the main woman in the SCLC office in Atlanta and it was very significant that she wanted to be present in Mississippi. The intimidation that the burning of the church was trying to deliver was something like, "Even your church—there is nothing you have that cannot be destroyed." James Chaney and Mickey Schwerner had been to the church a week earlier and Mickey spoke after the 11:00 service. And the church had agreed to host a Freedom School. And we knew that meant adult citizenship training would follow when we could get the adults to come out. That sort of training never would have been on Sunday morning, of course, and when we finally did get things started the Freedom Schools were on Saturdays in the churchyard, but just like Sunday school we would use the rooms.

Before this happened the Sixteenth Street Baptist Church in Birmingham had been bombed. So there had been previous horrors, but still this was the first bombing of this sort in Mississippi. The bombing started in Miami and slowly spread. It started in Miami because the NAACP people there in the early 1950s were doing voter registration and standing up. In Mississippi we were late in getting at that particular kind of violence. But we eventually had more bombing than anyone else. The violence slowly spread across the Deep South because people were doing voter registration and standing up. The bombing came everywhere black people stood up. I say bombing, but Mt. Zion church may have been just burned. They may have just thrown gasoline on it and so on. Later there were actual bombs and dynamite.

—*Rev. Edwin King, interview by Trent Watts, June 2, 2009, transcript, December 2009, transcript in author's possession.*

Neshoba was typical of the new territory COFO hoped to open in Freedom Summer, using an established movement base in a nearby city, Meridian, in this case. In Neshoba County, Mt. Zion was the only facility that was open to the movement . . . On June 16 the Klan (including uniformed white police) surrounded the church at the end of a business meeting. They demanded to know where the guns were hidden and brutally beat church leaders, threatening to kill one man unless he revealed the guns. He lost consciousness and his wife dragged him away. Initial COFO reports say he suffered severe jaw injuries, another man had a broken arm, and another a broken leg. The church was torched.

—*Ed King, "Neshoba," 4. Unpublished manuscript in author's possession.*

27. Press at Mt. Zion Church, July 1964—Neshoba, Miss.

Our strange little caravan drove far out into the country, deep into the forests along dirt roads, with the only homes being those of the black families who had owned their own small farms for a century. Then we reached the area called Longdale, not even a small town or crossroads. Here we gathered at the ruins of Mt. Zion. Probably nothing had changed in the few weeks since Mickey, Andrew, and James stood at the edge of the blackened ruins and twisted sheets of metal, probably from the roof. The burned bell was visible. No walls or fragments were standing. There was not much dust; perhaps summer rains had washed that away. The grass, bushes, and nearby trees were damaged, but already, in the Mississippi summer, nature was reviving and new green pushing against the ashes. By this time in the summer I had already seen the ruins of other burned churches, but this was still awful . . . and awesome. Last fall I had stared at the bomb-blasted church in Birmingham. This time, like then, I knelt and gathered shards of glass, twisted nails, relics. We should have removed our shoes for this soil we trod was holy ground.

Even the black preachers with us had little to say. Dr. King tried to say something about the significance of churches: "I feel sorry for those who were hurt by this . . . I rejoice that there are churches relevant enough that people of ill will are willing to burn them. This church was burned because it took a stand." I wept as Martin led us in prayer as we stood in the middle of the ruins of Mt. Zion.

—Ed King, "Testimony From Mt. Zion," 3–4. Unpublished manuscript in author's possession.

Before Chaney, Schwerner, and Goodman were killed, the necessary contacts with the federal government were made by COFO, the pleas for help were made—and ignored. The Jackson COFO office first contacted the FBI and then the Justice Department. Meridian COFO also made contacts with a lawyer from Justice already in their town. These three contacts were with federal men in Mississippi. As later information in the trials of the accused Klansmen showed, the killings did not occur until much later that night, after the time of these initial federal contacts. We begged for help. Our government's men assumed we were just paranoid or interested in publicity. But the Justice Department must have known the reality of Mississippi—whatever the FBI thought or cared. The first contact was with the FBI. The FBI had agents in Meridian that night who were already investigating the Mt. Zion church bombing and brutality; the murders were carried out a little over twenty-five miles up the road from the motel where the FBI men stayed. Like most COFO people, I believe that the FBI could have prevented the Neshoba murders. Probably a simple phone call to the Neshoba sheriff or deputy or to the Philadelphia jail seeking information on the missing men would have shown the interest and concern of the federal government and been sufficient to shake the confidence of the Klansmen and to deter their plans. Even this was not done.

—Ed King, "Neshoba," 7–8. Unpublished manuscript in author's possession.

28. SCLC tour at Mt. Zion Church ruins, Neshoba Co., July 1964

My more paranoid thoughts may be understandable: I think some in the FBI believed there was "trouble" possible when we begged for federal help, but thought that the "trouble" would "only" amount to some whippings, which the agitators needed; such "trouble" might well scare off most of the rest of the summer volunteers. I do think the FBI, especially, and much of the rest of Washington wanted the Freedom Summer project halted. The Governor's Mansion in Jackson and the White House both wanted racial problems handled by experts, politicians. Many powerful persons in Washington, in Jackson, and in the Ku Klux Klan believed that Communists were behind, and in the front ranks, of the civil rights movement. Given the amount of Klan activity in the Deep South for years, including the murders in Mississippi, the mobs attacking the Freedom Riders, and the Birmingham church bombings, the level of FBI "infiltration" of various KKK groups was high and it is not unreasonable to wonder if the FBI did not also have advance knowledge of a plot to kill the three men.

Dealing with representatives of the FBI and of the Justice Department in Mississippi was so frustrating that COFO asked the Atlanta SNCC office to contact Washington. John Doar of the Justice Department was called, probably at about the very time of night the three men were standing beside the road, near the red clay bank, facing their captors, and death. It is possible that Doar and the Justice Department in Washington actually even knew of the missing men, and the fears of COFO, before the killings did take place. Doar said he was concerned and suggested that we seek help from the Mississippi Highway Patrol!

The three men were left alone in Neshoba. Many, many people knew what might happen to them. No help came. Their government did not help them. And so they died. The American government, particularly the Justice Department, and most especially the FBI, must forever bear part of the responsibility, the guilt, the shame, for the killings in Neshoba.

For those of us who were old movement veterans in COFO or CORE and SNCC, this was something that we would never forget. For most of the American college students, the summer volunteers, the attitude of their government was almost inconceivable. By the middle of 1964, few of us in the movement expected anything better from our government. We did have hope; it hurt to have our worst fears confirmed. We were not surprised at the government's inaction in Neshoba. As many of the summer volunteers grew beyond surprise to understanding, the failure of their government was something they, too, would never forget.

—Ed King, "Neshoba," 8–10. Unpublished manuscript in author's possession.

29. Neshoba, '64—July, Mt. Zion beating victim [Roosevelt Cole] talks to C. T. Vivian of SCLC

Obviously the sheriff would have been interested in what we were doing. He certainly would have had authority to follow us anywhere we went. But I do not remember sort of looking over our shoulders constantly that day. The main road is down in here, though, and there were plenty of places they could have parked near us just to watch what we were doing. And everywhere I went for three or four years, I would say 95 percent of the time I was followed by police. So being followed would have been very normal. However, I do not remember thoughts like those when we left here go to see Mr. and Mrs. Roosevelt Cole . . . I do not remember being worried whether or not the police would be there. Our concern was would there be somebody in the woods. Once we had gotten there a couple hours earlier and nobody had attacked us and we saw these police guarding the intersection, we would have felt a little more comfortable. And Martin Luther King is so prominent a figure that they certainly are not going to make a false arrest with newsmen and other things around. We presumed that the governor had put out orders that nothing should happen and probably the president, too.

—Rev. Edwin King, interview by Trent Watts, June 2, 2009, transcript, December 2009, transcript in author's possession.

From Mt. Zion we drove further down the dirt road to the nearby home of Junior Roosevelt (Bud) Cole, church lay leader, and his wife, Beatrice. Bud Cole was an independent farmer, owning a small plot of about six acres of cotton; Beatrice Cole was a schoolteacher. They had ten children. The Coles told their story to Dr. King, just as they had told it a few weeks earlier to James Chaney, Andrew Goodman, and Mickey Schwerner, as told to other COFO workers, and as told, in full detail, to FBI agents, several days before our three men had come. The Coles were the last known contact with our men who had interviewed them, headed home, and disappeared. Mrs. Beatrice Cole did most of the talking. Mr. Bud Cole still suffered from injuries, including a broken jaw, received in the Klan beating. The Mt. Zion church was the only church in the county open to the movement. Bishop Charles Golden, a few months earlier, had called for all Methodist churches to be open to the civil rights movement, that is, the black churches of the Central Jurisdiction of the Methodist Church. Mt. Zion accepted the bishop's call and the call of the movement and agreed to host both a Freedom School and voter registration meetings and mass meetings. Chaney and Schwerner had visited there several times that spring and Mickey had made an impassioned appeal at the Sunday service at the end of May. Bud Cole was a church officer and Beatrice Cole the voter registration worker.

On June 16 after a routine board of stewards meeting ended around 9:00 p.m. the people came outside to find themselves surrounded. A mob of white men had blocked all road exits from the church. Several black men were terribly beaten and Bud Cole was clubbed unconscious. Beatrice Cole told us the story. Dr. King and the rest of us listened to her words, which sounded like scripture.

"They [the white men] stopped us not far from the church and one of the men had some words with my husband. There was at least twenty of them. Then one of them pulled my husband out of the car and beat him, I couldn't see with what, but it looked like an iron object. Then they kicked him while he was lying on the ground. Then they said to him, 'Better say something or we'll kill you.'"

—Ed King, "Testimony From Mt. Zion," 4–5. Unpublished manuscript in author's possession.

30. Neshoba Co., Miss., July 1964, SCLC trip—people describe beating at Mt. Zion Church of Neshoba, Andy Young—SCLC, Annelle Ponder—SCLC/COFO

Mrs. Cole continued:

"I said, 'He can't say nothing, he's unconscious.' Then I began to pray . . . I was praying very hard. I was just praying, saying, 'Lord have mercy, Lord have mercy, don't let them kill my husband.' And then I heard a voice sound like a woman scream down the road just a little piece below me and then a man walked up with a club and I continued saying 'Lord have mercy' and he drew back to hit me and I asked this policeman that was standing by him would he allow me to pray and this one was on the right and one was on the left. The one on the right says if you think it will do you any good you had better pray. The one on the left says it is too late to pray. They told me to shut my mouth. But I said, 'Let me pray.'

"I stretched out my hands. I fell on my knees and began to pray, and as I prayed I just said, 'Father, I stretch my hands to Thee, I stretch my hands to Thee, no other help I know. If Thou withdraw Thyself from me, whither can I go?' That struck the hearts of those men. The Lord was there. Because then the man said, 'Let her alone,' and he looked kind of sick about it."

Mrs. Cole's husband had not regained consciousness during this. She then told of one of the white men raising the butt of his gun to hit her and another white man interjecting, "Don't touch her . . . You might as well let them live." She was finally able to arouse her husband and the white men let them get in their car and leave. The white men stayed at the church. From her home down the road, out of sight of the church, she looked back at a terrible red glow in the night sky, "a lot of light coming up from around the church." The next morning she did visit the still-smoking ruins.

She also told us of two very important earlier visits:

"Those three boys . . . the same ones that are missing, came here on Sunday, June 21, they stayed about twenty minutes and left in the middle of the afternoon. The white boy with the beard I saw at that meeting at the church a couple of weeks ago when they talked about setting up a special school . . . The FBI was here the Friday after the church burned down and asked us questions about it."

That was a damnable statement about the FBI. I had learned this in COFO reports, but it still hurt to hear this lady's remark. The FBI, even with knowledge of this terrorism, two days later refused to help when COFO reported the men as missing. My government let my friends be killed.

—Ed King, "Testimony From Mt. Zion," 6. Unpublished manuscript in author's possession. See also Florence Mars, Witness in Philadelphia (Baton Rouge: Louisiana State University Press, 1977), 169–170.

31. Neshoba, Miss. [Beatrice Cole], Mt. Zion beating described to M. L. King, lady says she prayed and Klan did not kill her or her husband

My bitter thoughts were broken when Beatrice Cole closed this testimony of faith with a very funny comment about how the white policemen and Klansmen had treated the black men so terribly and questioned the men about political activities, but didn't ask her too many questions, and that she, the woman, was the one with the political information on the Mississippi Freedom Democratic Party and the one doing the voter registration work. But they didn't quite suspect a woman as a leader. They did make an effort to search her purse, but she told them that all she had was Sunday school literature; the MFDP leaflets were never discovered. How could a woman be a political agitator?

Dr. King and the rest of us sort of laughed at this little story. We needed something light. We had come to comfort her, to show that we stood with the local people. But this Christian woman, with her powerful testimony of faith, had brought comfort and strength to us. And we were blessed.

Beatrice Cole later told a friend, Florence Mars, one of the few whites in Neshoba trying to discover and face the Klan violence, that the words of her prayer were from an old Methodist hymn. "That song always have cherished me. The Devil was sponsoring that group, but the Lord was there."

We left Neshoba and drove on down to Meridian. We ended the day in a room in Charles Young's hotel in Meridian, exhausted, sad, frightened, but laughing at some of the absurdity and at ourselves, as we quickly got out of our sweaty suits and sat around in underwear with beer and Cokes to cool us and a small electric fan spreading its circle of breeze. Our comments bordered on the silly, the profane, but we had all wondered whether we would live through the afternoon. Our jokes about things that had frightened us became our kind of Te Deum.

—Ed King, "Testimony From Mt. Zion," 7–8. Unpublished manuscript in author's possession.

32. Rural Miss. scene, Neshoba County, black washing kettle

This photo must have been taken beyond the road between the Mt. Zion church and Roosevelt Cole's house. It may even have been at the Coles' place. Now, the Coles eventually got a small brick house. They're dead now, but I took church leaders up to meet them for thirty years. Their house then was a clapboard wooden house, not a Delta dogtrot house, but the type of house common among the east Mississippi rural poor. The washtub over an open fire and washboard was part of the texture of life for rural black Mississippi. You'd need a mule around somewhere, but this is the way of life for small farmers in the hills and in the piney woods. They may have shared mules with other people. But that washtub certainly wasn't put out there for anything touristy.

—*Rev. Edwin King, interview by Trent Watts, June 2, 2009, transcript, December 2009, transcript in author's possession.*

As the Freedom Summer approached, the dominant mood of the society sometimes seemed absurd, sometimes insane, sometimes quite logical—once you had accepted some paranoid fantasy. One important mood was fear, chiefly fear

One of our reasons for having the Freedom Summer project was our conviction, proved through effort and experience (such as the segregated churches and arrests in the past year), that there would be no significant response to the racial crisis from any white moderates in Mississippi, including the leadership of the Christian churches.

[That summer] I had a long conversation with the Roman Catholic leader, Bishop Gerow, a kind and wise man, about seventy years old. He accepted my story that massive violence now faced Mississippi, that the Klan had revived and was assisted by law officials, that things had already moved from church burning to murder. Then Father Bernard Law, the editor of the diocesan newspaper and one of the few resident liberals in the state, counterattacked.* Law, in his early thirties, was educated at Harvard, but did not look with sympathy on the idea of Harvard students or any other "outsiders" coming into the state to work with the civil rights movement. Law favored desegregation, but with the right, responsible people setting the pace. He strongly disapproved of the movement concept of the need for confrontation and direct action.

Fr. Law heard part of my talk with the bishop and intervened at the point where the bishop was expressing his concern that if what I said about violence and murder were true, then the white church leadership of the state would have to do something to stop the violence. Law told the bishop that I was exaggerating—like civil rights workers do—that I was, understandably, emotionally upset, that I had been through too much during the past year, that I was wrong about Neshoba. Specifically, Law said that he knew for a fact that no church had been burned in Neshoba County . . . Law claimed to have checked with church leaders in Neshoba who assured him that no Negro church had been burned. Since I was obviously wrong about my story that my friends had been investigating a church burning when they disappeared, I was just as obviously wrong that they had been murdered . . . Reason and liberalism prevailed; sadly, I left.

—Ed King, "Neshoba," 18–19. *Unpublished manuscript in author's possession.*

---

* Law later served as bishop of Springfield and Cape Girardeau, Missouri, and as a cardinal in Boston and the Vatican.

34. Aug. '64, Jackson, Miss., MFDP Conv., Speaker—Henry, Guyot, Platform—Ella Baker, Joe Rauh

This photograph is taken at the black Masonic temple about a block from the COFO office. I think that the time is about two weeks after Martin's trip. These people are the Mississippi Freedom Democratic Party delegates; they are seated by counties. This is the first political participation for most of the people you see here. And I would say 75 percent of them had failed the voter registration test. In some counties we might not have had enough courage to actually go down and take the test, but most of the people that did the Freedom Democratic Party registration stuck with things through weekly meetings. By this time you had had a precinct meeting, then you had organized a county meeting, then you had organized a congressional district meeting, all the while teaching people each time that at each step they elect delegates to go further. Finally they have elected delegates to go to a national convention. All the while too they are learning about democracy. I mean, even in their churches and schools they were not familiar with the democratic process. The PTA in the black school would have been just a tool for fundraising of the principal who was controlled by a white superintendent. And while many of the churches would have a kind of democracy (if they were Baptists) of voting, the reality is that the Baptist preacher had almost more authority than a monsignor in a big Roman Catholic church. We were starting at the level of things like what are committees? What we were teaching was the most basic grammar school stuff about democracy. But it had been deliberately and systematically excluded from black education, and from their lives.

We would talk about if you elected somebody what do they do, what does the governor do, what does a senator do in Washington, why don't you think the president knows what you are saying? It is because you do not have a representative in Washington. But we would quickly get it down to the idea that the school board election is just as important as a U.S. senator. Sure, the sheriff might treat you a little kinder if you had a black sheriff. But you can get a better algebra book in your school if you have a black school board member. So we would try to get it as close to home as possible so that they could see where the vote could make a difference in their lives.

—Rev. Edwin King, interview by Trent Watts, June 2, 2009, transcript, December 2009, transcript in author's possession.

35. Aug. 1964, Jackson, Miss., MFDP Conv.

Let me say a word about the black middle class. The black middle class, the few of them there were, were proud that they could vote, that they were the middlemen and middlewomen in their communities and had very important roles. We, however, were a threat to the old order. Many of those people criticized the Freedom Vote in 1963, even though Aaron Henry himself was middle class and educated. I mean there were certainly people from the educated black middle class that stuck with the movement; Mrs. Devine, for instance, and Mrs. Gray and so on. Most of the black middle class, though, thought that we were wasting time with the Freedom Vote. They wanted to vote in what they thought of as the real election, where most of them had been voting Republican. They didn't want to waste their vote. They told us that and they also told us that what we were doing seemed silly. Charles Evers would mock us. Many of those black middle-class people would not come out to the precinct meetings where they might have been able to vote in the actual Democratic precincts; they knew it wasn't considered their business. When we had our meetings they did not come to those, either. In the last week or so after we announced there would be a state convention, Aaron Henry told me he had people calling him from all over and I even had people call me as a college teacher at Tougaloo. Middle-class people who now wanted to be in were calling and asking to participate. A number of them said something to the effect of who are these people who say they are running things in our county? Most of them are not even high school graduates! I would try to find spots for a few of those middle-class latecomers, but most of these delegates you see here are people with an eighth or ninth grade education. They are new to the process. They dress just like they are going to church.

And the attitude of much of the black middle class was a tension or an irritant to some that ran all the way through Atlantic City. For instance, for many people Mrs. Hamer was not the face they wanted associated with the movement. She is not what black middle-class and black professionals wished and believed black Mississippi to be. And that gets back to what whites had defined as what so-called respectable blacks should be. But the idea that if blacks could conform to that image, then they somehow would be accepted? That was a myth. A few would be accepted to a limited degree. In the world that existed, though, that limited degree was still better than anyone else. At least that's what people striving for that "re-spectability" seemed to believe.

—Rev. Edwin King, interview by Trent Watts, June 2, 2009, transcript, December 2009, transcript in author's possession.

36. Aug. 1964, Jackson, Miss., MFDP State Convention

S ome of the leadership of the MFDP was not as hopeful of success in Atlantic City as the rank and file delegates you see here. Certainly the leaders that were less hopeful would not have crushed the enthusiasm. But some of us would have been worried about how hurt people will be if this does not succeed. A couple of days before the convention I was given an assignment by Bob Moses to try to figure in advance where we might be blocked and what compromises might come and how we might respond. And I think I came up with over thirty different possibilities, but never the one that we did have offered to us. But at this level Bob was certainly thinking the same thing I was: how far can we go? Many of us had concluded that we were not going to be able to go all the way. But America might in fact respond positively, so we were not going to be hypocrites. I think a lot of the SNCC people who became so embittered after the convention had no idea that some of us who helped organize the party were seeing the possibility that we might not win this one. But many of us were trying to put this work in the context of this is one step and as soon as we are done with the convention we are going to start pushing the campaign and we have these laws on the books that work in our favor.

So even then the idea would have been that after the presidential election and the congressional challenge vote, we will go to the U.S. Congress and make our case for a new, supervised election. Under the Reconstruction laws that had never been taken off the books, Congress could indeed have supervised a new election. And of course we would have insisted that part of the supervision of that new election would have included supervision of registration. We had demonstrated that black Mississippians wanted to vote and we had also shown that the main obstacle to their voting was the abuse of the registration process by the county registrars of voters. We knew we would have to argue that point because Congress and most other Americans simply did not recognize the severity of the problem. If we could get that congressional supervision of a new election, it would be a little silly for Mississippi officials to proceed with fraud and intimidation with America watching. We came very close; the provisions that were being argued in Congress that summer about the Voting Rights Act did have the provision for federal supervision of voting and congressional review of the results. That achievement comes out of the MFDP, not out of the Selma march. The guts of that bill was our testimony about voter discrimination and intimidation that we sent to Congress from over one thousand Mississippians in September and October—starting with the people who had been to the convention—so when Congress passes the bill they do not want to say they are responding to people marching in Selma. The nation was, but Congress had grounds based upon solid legal stuff that we had been doing.

We were collecting affidavits through the summer of 1964. And we had hearings all around the state with local registrars subpoenaed under federal order. They had to testify in front of local black people. We had thousands of pages of documentation. Neither the rank and file delegates nor did most of us realize that Congress was in fact going to respond to this legal evidence and not just to the marches. You needed both, but these people would have been very optimistic, but when they were smashed, they were not pessimistic. They knew there were more steps. They were hurt, but not ready to quit. It was not the delegates here who became embittered. They knew what they were facing. The SNCC people who were already exhausted and who knew from civics lessons and everything what America ought to be like and how the government should be—these are the ones who felt let down. The very sophisticated kids from Berkeley and Harvard were some of the ones who became the most bitter.

—*Rev. Edwin King, interview by Trent Watts, June 2, 2009, transcript, December 2009, transcript in author's possession.*

37. Aug. 64, Jackson, Miss., MFDP St. Conv.

In a lot of places there was a conscious effort to get what we would now call a kind of gender equity in the delegations. We had to make sure there were some men. The women were freer to come forward. Annie Devine had been a schoolteacher, but in most cases, even in the Delta, the women might work in white homes, or do some cotton picking, but we learned very quickly that the women were freer than the men to take the risk. I am joking about there being a conscious effort for gender equity. However, we did realize that we had far more women than most politics of the period had. The sit-inners were youth and college students. Their parents were just as insulted by not being able to go to a movie house or get a cup of coffee, but most of the men didn't dare protest openly; they had just accepted—to one degree or another—their roles. So, in many places that summer there would have been a disproportionate number of women.

It is not that there was no danger of economic reprisals for women. This is the period still when registering to vote meant your name went in the newspaper. Mrs. Hamer is the one who tries to register to vote and she and her husband, Pap, are turned out of their house on the plantation. But we have no stories of his standing up and reading scripture to calm the people. I met him; he's dead now. He certainly supported the movement, but she was the one who was reaching out. And he was doing his thing maybe by being quiet, trying to keep things going.

—*Rev. Edwin King, interview by Trent Watts, June 2, 2009, transcript, December 2009, transcript in author's possession.*

There was one major uniting factor for everyone working on plans for the Freedom Summer—that the time for action had come. This separated the "movement" from more conservative civil rights forces (like the national NAACP and even some local "successful" black citizens of Mississippi). The liberal administration in Washington did not think that the summer of 1964, a presidential election year, was the time—and that anyone outside of Mississippi even had the right to decide when or if such a time should ever come. Because of the hard work of Al Lowenstein, many liberals accepted the idea that some major confrontation with Mississippi was needed, even in the summer of 1964. But among those who favored a summer program, there was little agreement on actual content and specific goals. The range of opinion extended from moralistic churchmen and optimistic liberals to pessimistic young blacks questioning if the time for violence had not come. In between was most of the full-time staff in Mississippi whose initial outlook was very practical—whatever needed to be done would just have to be done. In Mississippi that meant finding the right next step to take; resistance would be just as severe for big or small steps . . . Even the political challenges were well within the rules of the system.

—*Ed King, "Needles and Spears," 73. Evans B. Harrington Collection. (MUM00219). Box 14, Folder 9. The Department of Archives and Special Collections, J. D. Williams Library, The University of Mississippi, Oxford, Mississippi.*

38. Aug. 64, Jackson, Miss., MFDP St. Conv.

Here at the convention the speakers would have been congratulating the delegates on having come this far. They would have been saying standard political-type stuff, such as we are going to keep going, and we will win. Ella Baker gave a beautiful speech. Ms. Baker was the director of the Washington, D.C., office of the MFDP and the nationwide campaign to build support for the national convention. A veteran of decades of grassroots organizing. She had worked for the NAACP and SCLC; she was a model and mother for the founding of SNCC and its independent youth-led group after the 1960 sit-ins. She talked deeper about the sense of the movement and not the mechanics of what we were doing. This is when she said—you know the line I am talking about—"Until the killing of black men, black mothers' sons, becomes as important to the rest of the country as the killing of a white mother's son, we who believe in freedom cannot rest until this happens." She was letting us all know we were part of something infinitely bigger than we thought. We would also have been pushing Lyndon Johnson for reelection and our loyalty to the national party in contrast to the regular Democrats.

—Rev. Edwin King, interview by Trent Watts, June 2, 2009, transcript, December 2009, transcript in author's possession.

The alienation of white Mississippi Democrats from the national party had been going on for some time, of course, but especially during the Kennedy presidency and into the summer of 1964. Most of the black people of Mississippi regarded themselves as Democrats. They were glad to hear the Mississippi Democrats renounce any affiliation with the national party. The more the white candidates of both parties attacked the Democratic Party and President Kennedy, the more popular both became in the Negro communities. Since most black people could not vote and did not have to make a choice between the two conservative candidates, there was no problem convincing people that they should vote for the "third" party. [At the beginning], there was never an official name for this new party [that we launched in 1963], just the "Freedom Vote" or the "Aaron Henry for Governor Committee." But by late October [of 1963], many people were beginning to use their own phrase for our activities. This new term was "Freedom Party."

Because of the fear of white violence and/or arrests, it was not possible to hold public rallies in many places [in 1963]. Here the campaign just concentrated on convincing a minister or café operator that they should allow a ballot box to be placed in their church or store and allow a worker to be there during the election. Although some places where COFO had hoped to have Aaron Henry speak proved impossible (such as Yazoo City and Belzoni) there were many other communities that put aside their fear and did have a campaign rally. To promote attendance at the rally, COFO workers would canvass a black neighborhood, going door to door (often as a car of white police followed them). But soon Aaron Henry began to appear on the stump, like a traditional Mississippi politician, at outdoor rallies such as the "Fish Fry for Henry" in the yard of Mt. Olivet Church where over two hundred residents of Holmes County cheered their candidate and donated money for the campaign. The "Freedom Fish Fry" became a popular way of raising money among the poor for COFO, and later, the MFDP.

—Ed King, "1963 Freedom Vote," 62–63, 65. Evans B. Harrington Collection. (MUM00219). Box 14, Folder 6. The Department of Archives and Special Collections, J. D. Williams Library, The University of Mississippi, Oxford, Mississippi.

39. Jackson, Miss., Aug. 64, MFDP St. Conv.

I n the fall of 1963 and in the winter of 1964 men and women in the movement were willing to suffer, to risk death, for gains they thought would be
very small for as long as they could imagine in the future. Most of our efforts
centered around political organizing (the approved form of power in America)
as the best way to change the awful conditions of the black people of Mississippi
. . . The voter registration effort by the fall of 1963 had to be regarded as a massive
failure. But that very fall Bob Moses had led SNCC into establishing two new
SNCC literacy projects, in Selma, Alabama, and at Tougaloo, Mississippi. The goal
was to teach adult literacy; these projects were to develop teaching methods suit-
able to the black poor of the Deep South. Literacy was important in learning new
jobs, if such an opportunity ever developed; literacy was important to passing the
literacy test for voter registration, if such an opportunity ever developed. SNCC
staff working in this area of education were considered just as important a part of
the SNCC organization as the most daring worker in some other field. To accept
such an emphasis on education, one of the slowest means of social change, meant
that SNCC was beginning to understand time from the perspective of the older
people they worked with.

In terms of actual voter registration we had to talk about what might one day
be true. In the face of daily frustrations and pessimism, talk of the future was

reassuring. But the things we talked about were amazing, although I certainly did not realize it at the time. We talked of adding a few thousand people to the role of registered voters each year—for years and years to come! That was gradual-ism and we would have to fight to get that much. We spoke of the importance of running black candidates, who had no chance of winning an election, but whose very campaign could teach unregistered Blacks the meaning of political organiza-tion and stimulate voter registration efforts. The biggest numerical goal we could talk comfortably about was passing the 50,000 mark on registered voters (of the 450,000 eligible black citizens). This task might take the next few years. We hoped to be able to win a few elections in the rural, black majority districts by the late sixties. The black vote would increase so slowly that no serious effort on a large scale could be made until at least 1972, when we talked about Bob Moses run-ning a serious campaign for the U.S. Senate against Jim Eastland.* We figured we would still lose that election, but after that, things would turn in our favor. This was SNCC in 1963 talking about not seeing the fruits of their labor until 1973, a decade away. Beyond that, time still had no meaning.

—Ed King, "Needles and Spears," 84–85. Evans B. Harrington Collection. (MUM00219). Box 14, Folder 9. The Department of Archives and Special Collections, J. D. Williams Library, The University of Mississippi, Oxford, Mississippi.

---

* James O. Eastland was a U.S. senator from Mississippi in 1941 and again from 1943 until his retirement in 1978. He chaired the Judiciary Committee from 1956 until his retirement. See Christopher Myers Asch, *The Senator and the Sharecropper: The Freedom Struggles of James O. Eastland and Fannie Lou Hamer* (New York and London: The New Press, 2008).

40. Aug. 64, Jackson, Miss., MFDP Convention (Madison Co. delegation), Mrs. Annie Devine

W e certainly did not expect any political "victory" in the 1964 summer that would result in overnight changes in life in Mississippi. What we did want out of the 1964 summer was the kind of victory that would keep the movement alive (in hope and in work) in Mississippi, that would allow SNCC to believe that their slow work would some day bring results, and, above all, that would allow them to continue that work. The ultimate goal of the Freedom Summer was to make the work of organizing possible. Since 1961 SNCC had learned much about organizing, but done little—so much time and effort were spent staying alive and fighting repression. The only way this freedom to organize, this freedom to start the work for the long haul, could be achieved was by federal intervention. No appeal from black civil rights workers for justice could ever move Washington—but the white parents of white volunteers, their neighbors and their congressmen, just might be able to shake the federal government into action. The steps and the scope of the Freedom Summer program developed out of this logic. What was needed in federal intervention was two things: some degree of federal responsibility to guarantee the right to vote for black citizens; some degree of federal responsibility to control and limit the violence and harassment, by public officials and private citizens, against black people and civil rights workers.

Justice and reason would call for a total federal occupation of the state (and other parts of the South) and a new Reconstruction government. No one expected this to happen. But what we needed to see was a beginning of "law and order," that the federal government would at least make full use of the existing laws about voter registration and the protection of the rights of American citizens (even if not politically expedient). In truth what we needed to see was, for once, traditional political expediency set aside in favor of justice. We did not expect the federal government to protect the life of every black voter, of every civil rights worker in Mississippi on every occasion; but we did expect at least some protection for some people some of the time—so that any white man who contemplated a violent attack against us had to think twice.

—Ed King, "Needles and Spears," 86–87. Evans B. Harrington Collection. (MUM00219). Box 14, Folder 9. The Department of Archives and Special Collections, J. D. Williams Library, The University of Mississippi, Oxford, Mississippi.

41. Atlantic City, Aug. 1964, MFDP Headquarters, Miss. delegates arrive

Now this is really sort of the end of the story in several ways. This is the hotel where the FDP delegation stayed in Atlantic City. They had come up on a bus with food packs that people had prepared for them. They were worried, of course, that across Alabama, North Carolina, and all of that you may not even be able to stop for food. So again, there had been lots of local people seeing them off. I guess the buses gathered in Jackson or somewhere. I was already up there. And several of us had had a rally in New York City the day before I had flown up, I believe. The historian C. Vann Woodward spoke at a rally for the MFDP at Town Hall.

Many of the delegates you see here had never been out of the state. Then there were the national television cameras and the spectacle of the whole thing. The week after we got back, I heard Hartman Turnbow trying to describe it. And he was trying to describe going to some northern delegation in a hotel and the chandelier that he saw. And chandelier wasn't a word he knew, but there was nothing any of his people, this was in Holmes County, there was nothing he could even relate it to. He was quite famous for misquoting things and so on. He did a good enough job describing that chandelier, but it was unimaginable splendor. Those were some tired people you see there around the bus.

The story of what happened at the convention has been told many times. We arrived at Atlantic City in a mood of super confidence. We thought that we were going to win something, that we will have really done something. Soon, of course, we were disappointed, some of us very bitterly disappointed. But that had not happened yet. What you see in this collection of pictures, then, from Martin's visit to Jackson to the death of the Neshoba martyrs to our arriving in Atlantic City is a period with a mood of hope and expectation that the work and the sacrifice would deliver something—that the early SNCC efforts in the state and the work in the Freedom Vote of 1963 and Freedom Summer itself would bear fruit—that our nonviolent work within and against the system would pay off. In Atlantic City, Mrs. Hamer's eloquent testimony before the Credentials Committee, which was broadcast on television, we hoped would convince other delegates of the justice of our cause. Many among us did not know all that was working against us at the convention. Lyndon Johnson did not want Mrs. Hamer and a bunch of civil rights workers to distract from his convention. Hubert Humphrey offered us two seats—one for me and one for Aaron Henry. This was their attempt at a compromise. We had a true, democratically elected group of sixty-something delegates. And then there was the all-white Mississippi delegation. And as a compromise they offered us two "observer" seats. We hadn't come all that way for two seats.

—Rev. Edwin King, interview by Trent Watts, June 2, 2009, transcript, December 2009, transcript in author's possession.

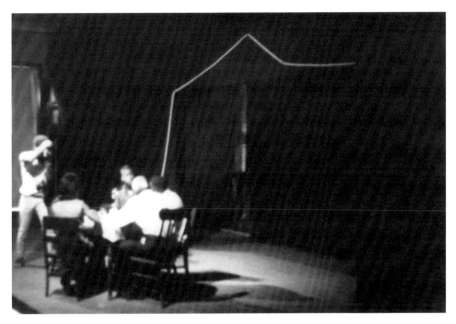

42. 1964 F. Summer, Toug., Miss., Play by Madison Co. Freedom School

While these are junior high and high school students performing here, the background and inspiration for this work was the Free Southern Theatre that was started at Tougaloo College the previous year. They performed at Tougaloo, of course, and also all around the state. John O'Neal of SNCC was director of that project. So that is why the students are doing this play of their own. With inspiration from the Free Southern Theatre, some of the Freedom Schools would have done their own plays. Jeannette King, my wife, was among the organizers and Freedom School teachers.

Local people wrote them. The place of the arts in movement work is not well enough known. For instance, a book of Freedom School poetry got reissued this past year by somebody in California. But whether theater or poetry, it's still the idea that we could be doing art and poetry and music or theatre with local people. The themes were mostly connected with the work that was going on or something like an incident from black history. The Free Southern Theatre did Becket's *Waiting for Godot* just because we believed people could talk about even the most far-out philosophy of our time. And they also did an off-Broadway comedy about plantation life in the 1950s with stuff that was a little bit more familiar; it had a Mr. Charlie character to be laughed at and so on. These people, these students would have been the next generation beyond the adults that would join the MFDP.

While I knew that the movement work was historic, most of the time I didn't have my camera with me. A million times I did not, but a few times certainly with Martin I did. But the work that summer was the primary thing. I did not have the presence of mind to ask Martin to sign a book when he was in my home for an MFDP strategy session wih Bayard Rustin and others about the Democratic convention. And I did have books by him. I knew that a lot of the student volunteers had expensive cameras and I knew other people were documenting and covering the work, but I sort of had a sense that there are some things I have seen that I want to preserve and remember. I was hoping I might have had a picture in here of a Freedom School in Camden, Mississippi, which is in Madison County. My family's history goes back a long way in Madison County. Camden is named for Camden, South Carolina, from which early settlers came when Mississippi was the frontier. My great-great-great-grandmother is buried there in Camden in Madison County; her husband fought in the Revolutionary War. Later, my mother's family had plantations and slaves in the area. And I remember going out there to Camden that summer because it really was isolated, but I do not think I had a camera with me. But I made a point to make the visit to check the morale there and of course I also felt like I was a minister and a chaplain to this whole group. I tried to visit many places. And I was an officer in the party, a temporary officer until we could elect permanent officers. But I sort of had a sense that I wanted to get some pictures of some of the other things.

Most of these photographs I took when I knew I wasn't going to be the speaker or something like that. These would have been taken with a 35 millimeter camera. I enjoyed photography. I like this one photograph even better because these are high school students and not the college students who were in the Free Southern Theatre. But that is what inspired them, and in a way that was our whole point.

—*Rev. Edwin King, interview by Trent Watts, June 2, 2009, transcript, December 2009, transcript in author's possession.*

Jeannette worked in the Freedom Schools; those schools were Charlie Cobb's idea. She had helped with the plans and excitement about the ideas and wanted direct participation in the summer program led by Staughton Lynd. Despite my fears, she worked in Canton, twenty miles away, in the school at the Asbury Methodist Church where Rev. James McCree was pastor. McCree was a major leader in the Madison County movement. Every weekday Jeannette made the trip through hostile territory.

One night Jeannette brought home a white volunteer, Nancy, who was from New York. She was sick and needed a quiet place to rest for a few days, so she moved into our back room. In the predawn hours she became quite ill. Dr. Robert Smith, Tougaloo College physician and doctor to the movement, diagnosed appendicitis and said Nancy was in critical condition. Jeannette rushed the woman to the University Medical Center Hospital, where her condition was recognized as, indeed, critical, perhaps life threatening. Immediate surgery was required.

Jeannette waited in the family area. After about ten minutes, hospital officials came to her with a crucial question: "Is Nancy colored or white?" Having come to the emergency room from Tougaloo College, hospital staff assumed their patient was Negro but now they were not sure. A white woman had brought her to the hospital. Before surgery could be done it was absolutely necessary that her race be ascertained.

Jeannette was furious and gave them hell. She refused to give the needed racial label; the hospital refused to proceed with the surgery. So Jeannette had to tell them the racial identity—and she also told them what she thought of their procedures. Nancy did receive excellent care and her life was saved.

This public hospital, supported with ample federal funds, had "white only" waiting rooms and other facilities. The other two available city hospitals, one supported by the Southern Baptists and the other by the Roman Catholic Church, also maintained segregated facilities.

Our home at Tougaloo College during Freedom School operated as a center for high-level strategy sessions, a guest house, and a rest home for ailing or exhausted COFO workers. Moments here were generally a delightful time. Early in the summer one white volunteer came to us with a serious problem. Soon enough that problem came directly into our living room.

This young man was Steve Bingham, who was based in the Delta and was working with Hollis Watkins and others in Holmes County. He had a strange story indeed. Steve explained that his grandfather had been a U. S. senator from Connecticut and this family was known and liked by Mississippi's own senators, Stennis and Eastland. Sen. Jim Eastland had discovered that the young Bingham was working in his own Delta country, a likely enough place for someone to be murdered or disappear. So Eastland arranged "protection" for Steve. Members of the state police, the white-only highway patrol, were assigned to guard (to watch?) Bingham at all times. So a white patrol car was parked outside the black home where he stayed in the Delta. White police followed him everywhere. Not only was this embarrassing, but it did make voter canvassing of black neighborhoods rather awkward.

Steve Bingham came to talk to us about the matter. His white police escorts followed him to the Tougaloo campus. To have a white police car on campus was dangerous for the police as well as all of us. Tougaloo students would regard such a "visit" as provocative. If word of the police presence spread on campus, students might attempt to rescue the COFO workers.

Steve introduced me to the two officers following him, and after a lengthy conversation I persuaded the officers to park near my house, but just off the campus. At my house Steve parked his car where the officers could see it. But that was not enough. His escorts had orders to watch Steve constantly. I promised not to sneak him off the campus but the police insisted on calling their headquarters. The orders came back. One of them had to keep watch and would have to follow Bingham everywhere, including the house (or den) of the notorious Ed King. The other officer would have to stay and guard the police car.

We accepted the situation. The man staying with the car placed two rifles in plain view of the windows. Then I persuaded him he would be much safer with the guns out of sight. I tried to get him out of the hot car, suggesting he sit in the shade of a nearby chinaberry tree and let us bring him a Coke. The other officer, a very young man with a typically gaunt white Mississippi frame, followed Bingham onto the infamous Tougaloo campus and even into our house.

Jeannette, ever the perfect southern hostess, did everything to make our surprise guest feel comfortable. Jane Stembridge, one of the earliest white southerners to join SNCC, helped with the hospitality, using her best Georgia drawl. Two black coeds seized the opportunity and helped with the entertaining, treating our guest as politely as if he were Dr. Aaron Henry.

The poor white policeman was in uniform. Soon Jane had him describing the various insignia and interesting bits of his costume. Then she began talking about his gun. Jeannette murmured that we did not usually have guests who wore guns in our living room. Jane kept asking questions and soon had the man remove his huge revolver from his waist belt and place it on our dining room table. He pulled his chair up closer to the gun and then accepted some iced tea and seemed to relax a little.

Jane asked about "all those big ole bullets in your belt." He spread a handful out on the table, telling us proudly that they were special for this summer. He explained that most Mississippi police were using much bigger guns this season with bullets that could kill a man almost every time. We were impressed.

While the ladies kept up the conversation Steve and I managed a few private words in another room, always reappearing often enough to reassure the officer. Steve placed some phone calls to the COFO office. The officer strained to listen but I turned up the noisy air conditioner and got him to tell me about those bullets.

Soon the party ended. Steve Bingham and company had to return to the Delta. The officer took a Coke and some cookies with him for the other officer as Jane smiled and said, "Bye, now." Then Jeannette added, "Y'all come back now, you hear?"

—Ed King. Unpublished manuscript in author's possession.

INDEX

Page numbers in **boldface** indicate photographs.

Canton, Mississippi, Freedom School in, 138

Capitol Street Methodist Church, attempt to integrate, 45n9

Carmichael, Stokely, 23, 58, 79

Carter, Bruce and Corey, 63

Carter, Hodding, Jr., 8

Central Jurisdiction (black Methodist conference), 12, 112

Chaffee, Lois, 43, 45n13, 70

Chaney, James: the Coles' meeting with, 112, 114; disappearance of, 54, 57, 91, 94, 105; funeral of, 23–24; locating body of, 96–98, 103; at Mount Zion Methodist Church ruins, 107; murder of, 22–23, 25, 90, 95–96; visit to Mount Zion Methodist Church, 106, 112. *See also* Neshoba County murders

Chickasaw County, Mississippi, registered black voters in, 27

Children, black, following MLK, **85**, 85–86, 94. *See also* Freedom Schools; Schools, integration of

Christmas, John, 15

Churches, black: bombings of, 75, 100; slow to become involved in civil rights movement, 77–78, 87. *See also individual churches*

Churches, white: Ed King's attempts to integrate, 15–16, 45n9; lack of response to racial crisis, 120. *See also individual churches*

Citizens' Council. *See* Mississippi: Citizens' Council

Citizenship education, 49, 52, 86, 106. *See also* Freedom Summer of 1964; Freedom Vote of 1963; Voter education; Voter registration

Civil Rights Act of 1964, 5

Civil rights movement: art's role in, 137; black Methodist Church leadership, 77–78; Communists associated with, 4, 7, 98, 102, 109; fear associated with, 43, 70, 130; fractures in, 8–9, 54; freedom song about dogs, 38, 44n7; Ed King's speeches on, 29; linking Vietnam War to, 104; media coverage of, 6, 30; number of people involved in, 82; racial reconciliation inspiring, 28;

significance of, 23–24; Tougaloo College students' involvement in, 13–17, 38, 45n9, 54; white violence against, 3–5, 7–8, 19, 22–25, 26; women's involvement in, 60, 64, 78, 127. *See also* Direct action campaigns; Freedom Riders; Freedom Rides of 1961; Freedom Summer of 1964; Freedom Vote of 1963; Nonviolence: civil rights movement's commitment to; Voter education; Voter registration

Civil rights workers, black: dogs used against, 45n8; lack of media attention toward, 24; leadership, 77; national government's lack of attention to, 133; white violence against, 26; working with whites, 60. *See also* Blacks; Neshoba County murders; Student volunteers, Freedom Summer; *individual workers*

Civil rights workers, white: Delta region, 19, 24, 51, 69, 139; Ed King's importance as, 6–8, 21–22; national government's failure to protect, 89–90, 96, 104, 114, 133–34; SNCC debates over using, 24, 54; white violence against, 3–5, 7–8, 14, 22–25, 26; working with blacks, 60. *See also* Neshoba County murders; Student volunteers, Freedom Summer; *individual workers*

Civil War, centennial of, 30

Clarion-Ledger, civil rights movement coverage of, 30

Clark, Robert, 18

Clarksdale, Mississippi, black voters in, 49

Class. *See* Middle class

Cobb, Charlie, 138

COFO. *See* Council of Federated Organizations

Cole, Beatrice, 117; MLK's meeting with, 111–14, 115, **115**

Cole, Roosevelt, **111**, **113**, 117; MLK's meeting with, 111–14, 115, **115**

Communists, associated with civil rights movement, 4, 7, 98, 102, 109

Congressional challenge, 75–76, 125–26

Congress of Racial Equality (CORE): break with SNCC, 26; challenging segregated transportation, 4; as COFO participant,

20; fractures within, 54; Freedom Riders affiliated with, 14; geographic area of responsibility, 57; interorganization work, 52; at MFDP strategy session, 81; MLK's meeting with, 52; the Schwerners' work for, 95; voter registration projects, 50, 68, 119

Cooper, Nancy, 138–39

CORE. *See* Congress of Racial Equality

Cotton, Dorothy, at Mount Zion Methodist Church ruins, **105,** 106

Cotton, Willie Mae, 74n

Council of Federated Organizations (COFO): break up of, 9, 266; the Coles' meeting with, 112; dangers faced by, 71; financial troubles, 68, 70; Freedom Summer goals, 26, 108; fundraising for, 130; Jackson office, 6, 49n, 57, 59–60, **61,** 68, 69–70, **73;** Ed King's work for, 21; and Neshoba County murders, 96, 104; requests for help from FBI and Justice Department, 90, 108, 109–10, 114; voter registration efforts, 52, 80, 130. *See also* King, Martin Luther, Jr.: at COFO's Jackson office

Danielson, Chris, 28

De La Beckwith, Byron, conviction of, 17, 30, 34n81

Delta region: black women working in, 127; Citizens' Council formed in, 4; dangers of interracial work in, 60, 64; dogs in, 41; MFDP popularity in, 18, 19; MLK's visit to, 81; poverty in, 28; voter registration efforts in, 5, 71; white civil rights workers in, 19, 24, 51, 69, 139

Democratic Party, 28, 53, 130. *See also* Johnson, Lyndon; Kennedy, John F.; Mississippi Freedom Democratic Party

Dennis, David, 19, 23

Devine, Annie, 123, 127, **133**; candidacy for U.S. Congress, 27, 76

Dialogue, interracial, 11, 25, 26

Direct action campaigns, 13–17, 20, 30, 50, 120, 128

Dittmer, John, 5, 7, 13, 19, 26

Doar, John, 109–10

Dogs, in Mississippi, 37–45; blacks', 37, 40, 41, 42, 43; children's love of, 38–40; fear of, 37, 39; obituaries for, 42–43; police, 15, 38, 39, 41–42, 45n8; whites', 37–38, 39, 40, 41, 42

Donald, Cleveland, 45n11

Eagles, Charles W., 4

East, P. D., 8

Eastland, James O., 23, 28, 132n, 139

Edwards, Don, 73–74

Edwards, Len, 74, **75**

Embry, Elroy, 12

Eubanks, W. Ralph, 29

Evers, Charles, 54, 82, 123

Evers, Medgar: and black boycott of state fair, 38; black Methodist churches open to, 78; and integration campaigns, 14, 16; interorganizational coordination efforts, 51, 52; Jackson airport named for, 30; Ed King's memorializing of, 29–30; murder of, 5, 16–17, 20, 65; as NAACP field secretary, 12; targeted by KKK, 22, 67

Evers, Myrlie, memoir by, 29–30

Farish Street Baptist Church (Jackson), Ed King's sermon at, 92

FBI. *See* U.S. Federal Bureau of Investigation

Fear: blacks' need to overcome, 38, 67, 92, 94, 100; civil rights workers', 43, 70, 130; of FBI, 97; Ed King's experiences of, 17; of police dogs, 37, 38–39; whites suffering from, 102, 117–18

Fisher, L. J., 42

Fondren, D. F., 42

Ford Foundation, 13

Fordice, Kirk, 25

For Us, The Living (memoir and film), 30

Frank, Barney, 21

Franklin, Marvin, 13

Freedom House (McComb), 73, 74; bombing of, 74n

Freedom Riders: arrests of, 5, 14, 38; honoring of, 63; police dogs used against, 38, 41; violence against, 4–5, 65

Freedom Rides of 1961: fiftieth anniversary of, 30; SNCC's participation in, 19

O'Brien, M. J., 15
Officeholders, black, 27, 28, 122, 132
Ogden, Florence Sillers, 45n10
Ole Miss. *See* University of Mississippi
O'Neal, John, 137

Parchman penitentiary, Freedom Riders held
    at, 5, 14
Parker, Mack, murder of, 20
Payne, Charles, 18, 20
Payne, Edwin, 42
Peacock, Willie, **83**
Philadelphia, Mississippi: danger in, 99;
    MLK's visit to, **81,** 81–82, **87,** 87–88; pool
    hall speech by MLK, **85, 87, 93,** 93–94, **95,
    99**; racial reconciliation in, 26, 125. *See
    also* Neshoba County; Neshoba County
    murders
Philadelphia Coalition, 25
Police, white, 139–40; attack on Mount Zion
    Methodist Church, 90, 106, 115; dogs
    used by, 15, 38, 39, 41–42, 45n8; Ed King
    harassed by, 92, 111; preserving Missis-
    sippi way of life, 21, 80, 102; surveillance
    of COFO office, 69–70; at Woolworth's
    sit-in, 15. *See also* Arrests
Ponder, Annelle, 52; at COFO's Jackson office,
    71; the Coles' meeting with, **113**; Winona
    jail beating, 53–54
Poverty, black, 10, 28, 88
Pratt Memorial Methodist Church (Jackson),
    49, **53**; MLK appearance at, **48, 51**
Primos, Aleck, 118
Protestant churches, 16, 77–78. *See also* Bap-
    tist churches, black; Methodist Church
Public awareness, raising: and denial of
    blacks' right to vote, 75–76, 80, 119; pres-
    suring federal government to intervene in
    Mississippi, 76, 133; and violence against
    blacks, 24, 27, 62, 84. *See also* Media cover-
    age

Quinn, Alynn, 72

Racism, 15, 24, 25, 92
Rauh, Joe, **121**

Reconciliation, racial, 25, 26, 27, 28, 31
Reconstruction laws, on voting, 76, 125–26,
    134
Reeves, Cecil, 42
Reuther, Walter, and MFDP's 1964 Demo-
    cratic National Convention challenge, 26
Ross, Benny, 39, 40
Rotwein, Abe, 42
Rustin, Bayard, 81, 138
Ryan, William Fitz, 73

Salter, John: automobile accident, 17; integra-
    tion campaigns, 13, 16; opposition to
    opening Sovereignty Commission papers,
    29; at Woolworth's lunch counter sit-in,
    14–15
Schools, integration of, 63, 86
Schwerner, Michael: civil rights work, 23, 57;
    the Coles' meeting with, 112, 114; disap-
    pearance of, 54, 57, 91, 94, 105; locating
    body of, 96–98, 103; murder of, 22–23,
    24, 25, 90, 95–96; visit to Mount Zion
    Methodist Church, 106, 107, 112, 114. *See
    also* Neshoba County murders
Schwerner, Rita, civil rights work of, 23, 57,
    80, 95, 96
SCLC. *See* Southern Christian Leadership
    Conference
Scott County, Mississippi, registered black
    voters in, 27
Segregation: of churches, 15–16; of hospi-
    tals, 139; Ed King's questioning of, 10, 11;
    preserving, 23; of schools, 63, 86; taken for
    granted by whites, 9–10, 11; of transporta-
    tion, 4–5; whites' defense of, 4, 45n10, 118.
    See also Jim Crow society; Mississippi:
    preserving whites' way of life in
Selah, W. B., 16
Self-defense, black, 57–58, 99–100. *See also*
    Nonviolence: civil rights movement's
    commitment to
Selma, Alabama: black voter drives, 26;
    march, 82, 126; SNCC literacy project, 131
Shirley, Dottie Lou (cousin), 39
Sillers, Walter, 45n10
Silver, James, 8